First World War
and Army of Occupation
War Diary
France, Belgium and Germany

61 DIVISION
Headquarters, Branches and Services
Royal Army Veterinary Corps
Assistant Director Veterinary Services
1 November 1915 - 31 March 1919

WO95/3041/4

The Naval & Military Press Ltd
www.nmarchive.com
Published in association with The National Archives

Published by

The Naval & Military Press Ltd

Unit 10 Ridgewood Industrial Park,

Uckfield, East Sussex,

TN22 5QE England

Tel: +44 (0) 1825 749494

www.naval-military-press.com

www.nmarchive.com

This diary has been reprinted in facsimile from the original. Any imperfections are inevitably reproduced and the quality may fall short of modern type and cartographic standards.

© Crown Copyright
Images reproduced by permission of The National Archives, London, England, 2015.

Contents

Document type	Place/Title	Date From	Date To
Heading	WO95/3041/3		
Heading	61st Division Asst Dir. Vety Services 1915 Sep Mar 1919		
Miscellaneous	Diary of Major Arnold Porritt	01/10/1915	01/10/1915
War Diary		01/11/1915	30/11/1915
Heading	War Diary of A.D.V.S 61st (South Mid.) Division From 1st December 1915 To 31st December 1915 Volume 2		
War Diary	Boreham	01/12/1915	31/12/1915
Heading	War Diary of A.D.V.S 61st (South Mid.) Division From 1st January 1916 To 31st January 1916 Volume 2		
War Diary	Boreham	01/01/1916	31/01/1916
War Diary	Havre	23/05/1916	24/05/1916
War Diary	St Venant.	25/05/1916	12/06/1916
War Diary	La. Gorge	13/06/1916	30/06/1916
War Diary	La. Gorgue	01/07/1916	27/10/1916
War Diary	St. Venant	28/10/1916	02/11/1916
War Diary	Chelers	03/11/1916	04/11/1916
War Diary	Roellecourt	05/11/1916	06/11/1916
War Diary	Frohen-Le-Grand	07/11/1916	14/11/1916
War Diary	Bernaville	15/11/1916	16/11/1916
War Diary	Canaples	17/11/1916	17/11/1916
War Diary	Contay	18/11/1916	22/11/1916
War Diary	Bouzincourt	23/11/1916	16/01/1917
War Diary	Marieux	17/01/1917	17/01/1917
War Diary	Bernaville	18/01/1917	19/01/1917
War Diary	Brailly	20/01/1917	05/02/1917
War Diary	Long	06/02/1917	14/02/1917
War Diary	Guillaucourt	15/02/1917	17/02/1917
War Diary	Harbonnieres	18/02/1917	28/02/1917
War Diary	Guizancourt	30/03/1917	12/04/1917
War Diary	Voyennes	13/04/1917	22/04/1917
War Diary	Auroir	23/04/1917	15/05/1917
War Diary	Vignacourt	16/05/1917	20/05/1917
War Diary	Doullens	21/05/1917	22/05/1917
War Diary	Le Cauroy	23/05/1917	23/05/1917
War Diary	Warlus	24/05/1917	02/06/1917
War Diary	Arras	03/06/1917	11/06/1917
War Diary	Warlus	12/06/1917	23/06/1917
War Diary	Willeman	24/06/1917	26/07/1917
War Diary	Zeggers Cappel	27/07/1917	15/08/1917
War Diary	Poperinghe	16/08/1917	18/08/1917
War Diary	Mersey Camp	19/08/1917	01/09/1917
War Diary	Watou	16/09/1917	18/09/1917
War Diary	Duisans	19/09/1917	24/09/1917
War Diary	G.17.a. Sheet 51.b.	26/09/1917	29/10/1917
War Diary	Arras	30/10/1917	30/11/1917
War Diary	Ytres	01/12/1917	01/12/1917
War Diary	Etricourt	02/12/1917	23/12/1917
War Diary	Mericourt	24/12/1917	31/12/1917
War Diary	Harbonnieres	01/01/1918	07/01/1918

War Diary	Nesle	08/01/1918	12/01/1918
War Diary	Auroir	13/01/1918	21/03/1918
War Diary	Rethonvillers	22/03/1918	23/03/1918
War Diary	Parvillers	24/03/1918	24/03/1918
War Diary	Beaucourt	25/03/1918	27/03/1918
War Diary	Villers Bretonneux	28/03/1918	28/03/1918
War Diary	Boves	29/03/1918	02/04/1918
War Diary	Pissy	03/04/1918	10/04/1918
War Diary	Aire	11/04/1918	18/05/1918
War Diary	Lambres	19/05/1918	14/07/1918
War Diary	Norrent Fontes	15/07/1918	22/07/1918
War Diary	Wardrecques	23/07/1918	01/08/1918
War Diary	I20.a.6.1. Sheet 36.A.	08/08/1918	31/08/1918
War Diary	Tannay	01/09/1918	09/09/1918
War Diary	Croix Marraisse	10/09/1918	06/10/1918
War Diary	Doullens	07/10/1918	09/10/1918
War Diary	Lagnicourt	10/10/1918	13/10/1918
War Diary	Noyelles Sur L'Escaut	14/10/1918	19/10/1918
War Diary	Rieux	20/10/1918	24/10/1918
War Diary	St Aubert	25/10/1918	26/10/1918
War Diary	Vendegies	26/10/1918	31/10/1918
War Diary	Bermerain	13/11/1916	13/11/1916
War Diary	Rieux	14/11/1918	14/11/1918
War Diary	Cambrai	15/11/1918	24/11/1918
War Diary	Bernaville	25/11/1918	30/11/1918
Miscellaneous	61st Division No A 36.	10/01/1919	10/01/1919
War Diary	St. Riquier	08/02/1919	24/03/1919
War Diary	Le. Treport	25/03/1919	31/03/1919

WO 95/3041/3

61ST DIVISION

ASST DIR. VETY SERVICES.

1915 SEP - MAR 1919

Subject:- Diary of Major Arnold Porritt
A.D.V.S.61st.(S.M.)Division
for, September,1915.

To:- Headquarters,61st.(S.M.)Division.

Wednesday,	1.	Accompanied Colonel Long Director of Remounts, with the inspection of the horses of the 61st.(South Midland) Division.
Thursday,	2.	Went to Ingatestone to interview Capt.C.Baxter,A.V.C. and inspect the horses belonging to the 2/3rd.S.M.R.F.A.
Friday,	3.	Interviewed Lieut.T.Batty A.V.C., and Mr.W.Scales C.V.S. re Central Force letter.
Saturday.	4.	Went to Thornwood Camp, Epping, to see Lieut.W.Bushnell A.V.C. of the 183rd. Inf Bde.
Sunday.	5.	Inspected the horses belonging to the 2/1 and 3/1., Signal Company.
Monday.	6.	Interviewed a Farmer at Chelmsford, concerning a Field being put out of bounds.
Tuesday.	7.	Inspected horses suspected with Mange belonging to the A.S.C. Chelmsford.
Wednesday.	8.	Interviewed by Colonel Walters A.D.V.S. 3rd. Army. Inspected Branch Veterinary Hospital, and A.S.C. horses.
Thursday.	9.	Went to Burnham on Crouch, to make arrangments for Mr.J.Sugden, M.R.C.V.S., to be a part-time C.V.S., with the 83rd.Provisional Battalion.
Friday.	10.	Went to Ingatestone, and inspected cast horses, of the 2/1 S.M.Bde R.F.A., also the 184th. Inf.Bde.
Saturday.	11.	Inspected cast horses, belonging to the Royal Berks at Chelmsford.,with Lieut T.Batty. A.V.C.
Sunday.	12.	Office work.
Monday.	13.	Inspected horses belonging to the 2/4 (How).R.F.A. at Baddow with Mr.W.Scales, C.V.S.
Tuesday.	14.	Went to Writtle to inspect the horses of the 2/2. S.M.R.F.A.
Wednesday.	15.	Went to Epping re cast horses, also inspected the horses of the A.S.C.Chelmsford.
Thursday.	16.	Inspected cast horses at Baddow, and made arrangements for Sale, also interviewed the Land agent re Brownings.

Diary of Major Arnold Porritt, (continued)

Friday.	17.	Went to the Sale of Horses at Chelmsford.
Saturday.	18.	Visited Mr.Young, M.R.C.V.S. and Mr.Upton, M.R.C.V.S., under 3rd. Army instructions.
Sunday.	19.	Oaklands Hospital, to see Lieut.W.Bushnell, A.V.C., who has had an accident.
Monday.	20.	Branch Veterinary, Hospital, also inspected horses belonging to the A.S.C.
Tuesday.	21.	Went to Maldon to see Mr.A.H.Brooks, C.V.S., also inspected horses for casting at Baddow.
Wednesday.	22.	Visited Mr.J.Sugden, C.V.S. at Southminster., also went to Oaklands Hospital to see Lieut.W.Bushnell,A.V.C.
Thursday.	23.	Went to Danbury, to make inquiries re Lieut.W.Bushnell's accident.
Friday.	24.	Went to Leamington Veterinary Hospital, to make inquiries re horses sent to Chippenham with mange.
Saturday.	25.	(At Leamington Veterinary Hospital.) Lieut.R.HH.Over A.V.C., in charge, inspected horses at Boreham, and duty at Brownings. A.D.V.S. returned to duty.
Sunday.	26.	Went to Epping to interview Mr.Upton, M.R.C.V.S., re account for feeding horses.
Monday.	27.	Inspected horses belonging to the A.S.C., also went to the Branch Veterinary Hospital.
Tuesday.	28.	Inspected horses suspected with mange and ringworm, belonging to the 2/2. R.F.A. Gt.Baddow.
Wednesday.	29.	Went to Epping to inspect the horses of the A.S.C., and the 183rd. Infantry Brigade.
Thursday.	30.	Interviewed Mr. Upton, M.R.C.V.S., also inspected the horses belonging to the 2/3.S.M.Bde R.F.A., at Epping.

Boreham House,
Chelmsford.
1st.Oct. 1915.

Arnold Porritt
Major,
A.D.V.S.61st.(South Midland)Division.

CONFIDENTIAL

Army Form C. 2118.

WAR DIARY
or
INTELLIGENCE SUMMARY.
(Erase heading not required.)

Instructions regarding War Diaries and Intelligence Summaries are contained in F. S. Regs., Part II. and the Staff Manual respectively. Title pages will be prepared in manuscript.

Hour, Date, Place	Summary of Events and Information	Remarks and references to Appendices
November 1st	Made arrangements for the Mobile Vety Section, which	
" 2	Came from Churn to Chelmsford.	
" 3	Inspected the Sick Mo Horses and took Temperature.	
" 4	Accompanied Col. Walters A.D.V.S 3rd Army to inspect the Horses of the Vets. Offr. at Hospital. Visited Oaklands Hospital, and posted Lieut. A. Thorne A.V.C. to do Veterinary Duty.	
" 5	Instructed by 3rd Army, to make arrangements for 82 Mange Cases to come to Chelmsford, or near by.	
" 6	Accompanied Col. Long Director of Remounts with the inspection of Horses	
" 7	Visited Branch Veterinary Hospital, Chelmsford.	
" 8	Inspected Horses with Col. Long Director of Remounts.	

Army Form C. 2118.

WAR DIARY
or
INTELLIGENCE SUMMARY.
(Erase heading not required.)

Instructions regarding War Diaries and Intelligence Summaries are contained in F. S. Regs., Part II. and the Staff Manual respectively. Title pages will be prepared in manuscript.

Hour, Date, Place	Summary of Events and Information	Remarks and references to Appendices
November — Continued		
9	Inspected Horses with Col. Long, C.B. Director of Remounts	
10	Inspected Horses with Col. Long, C.B. Director of Remounts	
11	Inspected Horses of the Beds. Yeo. (Went on Leave) Lieut. Oliver. A.V.C. acting A.D.V.S.	
12	Lieut. Oliver acting A.D.V.S. went to Ingates to inspect Horses from the West Somerset Yeo.	
13	Inspected by 3rd Army to go to Olney. Bucks, and inspected Sick Horses that were left by the Beds Yeo.	
14.	Branch Veterinary Hospital, Chelmsford.	
15	Heavy Correspondence, and Veterinary Hospital.	
16	Accompanied Col. Long. C.B. Director of Remounts with the inspection of Horses belonging to Royal Engineers.	

Forms/C. 2118/10

Army Form C. 2118.

WAR DIARY
or
INTELLIGENCE SUMMARY.
(Erase heading not required.)

Instructions regarding War Diaries and Intelligence Summaries are contained in F.S. Regs., Part II. and the Staff Manual respectively. Title pages will be prepared in manuscript.

Hour, Date, Place	Summary of Events and Information	Remarks and references to Appendices
	Continued.	
November 17	A.D.V.S. returned to duty. Attended to correspondence and inspected Horses of the A.S.C.	
" 18	Went to Dunman to interview Col. Walters. C.D. A.D.V.S. 3rd Army.	
" 19	Went to Bedford with Lieut Campbell, Dir. Director of Remounts, to inspect Cast Horses of Beds. Yeo.	
" 20	Inspected Horses of the A.S.C. Chelmsford.	
" 21	Attended to correspondence	
" 22	Inspected Horses at the First Aid Dressing Stations, and Mobile Vety. Sections	
" 23	Inspected Horses for casting belonging to the 184th Infantry Brigade.	

(9 29 6) W 4141—463 100,000 9/14 H W V Forms/C. 2118/10

Army Form C. 2118.

WAR DIARY
or
INTELLIGENCE SUMMARY.
(Erase heading not required.)

Instructions regarding War Diaries and Intelligence Summaries are contained in F. S. Regs., Part II. and the Staff Manual respectively. Title pages will be prepared in manuscript.

Hour, Date, Place		Summary of Events and Information	Remarks and references to Appendices
November	24th *Continued*	Went to Ingatestone, with Col. Walters, A.D.V.S. 3rd Army, to inspect mange cases, sent from the West Somerset Yeo. and North Devon Hussars, to the 31st S.M. Bde. R.F.A.	
"	25	Inspected Mr. W. Scales M.C.V.S. concerning the 7th & 8th Provisional Bde. R.F.A.	
"	26	Inspected Horses for Casting, belonging to the A.S.C.	
"	27	Inspected Horses for Casting belonging to the 184th Infantry Brigade.	
"	28	Inspected Horses for Casting belonging to the A.S.C.	
"	29	Accompanied Col. Walters A.D.V.S. 3rd Army, with the inspection of all the Horses of the 2/1st (South Mid.) Bde. R.F.A. Ingatestone.	

/ Army Form C. 2118.

WAR DIARY
or
INTELLIGENCE SUMMARY.
(Erase heading not required.)

Instructions regarding War Diaries and Intelligence Summaries are contained in F.S. Regs., Part II. and the Staff Manual respectively. Title pages will be prepared in manuscript.

Hour, Date, Place	Summary of Events and Information	Remarks and references to Appendices
Continued		
November 30	Posted Lieut Heath, A.V.C. to take over Veterinary duty of the Horses belonging to the A.S.C. and the 184th Infantry Bde, in the place of Lieut J. Batty A.V.C., who is on sick leave, pending transfer to Southminster.	
Boreham House Chelmsford.	Arnold Pratt Major. A.D.V.S. 61st (South Mid) Division	

CONFIDENTIAL.

WAR DIARY OF

A.D.V.S. 61ST (SOUTH MID) DIVISION.

FROM 1ST DECEMBER, 1915, TO 31ST DECEMBER, 1915.

Volume 2.

Army Form C. 2118.

WAR DIARY
OF A.D.V.S 61st (S.M) DIVISION
INTELLIGENCE SUMMARY.
(Erase heading not required.)

Place	Date	Hour	Summary of Events and Information	Remarks and references to Appendices
BOREHAM	1.12.15		Inspected horses at BADDOW	A.P.
"	2.12.15		Posted Mr. W. SCALES, C.V.S., to take the place of Capt. CADE, A.V.C., who is on sick leave.	A.P.
"	3.12.15		Inspected horses with mange at INGATESTONE, with Col. RUTHERFORD, G.B., D.D.V.S., General Jones	A.P.
"	4.12.15		Nil	A.P.
"	5.12.15		Inspected horses at CHELMSFORD.	A.P.
"	6.12.15		Inspected horses at BRENTWOOD	A.P.
"	7.12.15		Visited 1st Aid Veterinary Station, CHELMSFORD	A.P.
"	8.12.15		Inspected horses at BRENTWOOD	A.P.
"	9.12.15		Inspected horses at CHELMSFORD.	A.P.
"	10.12.15		Inspected stables at INGATESTONE HALL.	A.P.
"	11.12.15		Nil	A.P.
"	12.12.15		Inspected sick horses at INGATESTONE, with Col. WALTERS, A.D.V.S. 3rd Army.	A.P.
"	13.12.15		Inspected Remounts at CHELMSFORD	A.P.
"	14.12.15		Inspected mange cases at the 1st Aid Veterinary Station, CHELMSFORD.	A.P.

Army Form C. 2118.

WAR DIARY
of A.D.V.S. 61st (S.M) DIVISION
INTELLIGENCE SUMMARY
(Erase heading not required.)

page 2.

Instructions regarding War Diaries and Intelligence Summaries are contained in F.S. Regs., Part II. and the Staff Manual respectively. Title pages will be prepared in manuscript.

Place	Date	Hour	Summary of Events and Information	Remarks and references to Appendices
BOREHAM.	15.12.15		Inspected mange and ringworm cases at INGATESTONE.	A.P.
"	16.12.15		Interviewed Col. WALTERS, A.D.V.S., 3rd Army, DUNMOW.	A.P.
"	17.12.15		Instructed by 3rd Army, to go to SOUTHEND, SOUTHMINSTER, BRADWELL, BURNHAM, and CLACTON, to inspect horses of Provisional Brigades.	A.P.
"	18.12.15		Inspected Remounts at CHELMSFORD	A.P.
"	19.12.15		Nil	A.P.
"	20.12.15		Inspected horses at CHELMSFORD	A.P.
"	21.12.15		Inspected horses at STOCK, and INGATESTONE.	A.P.
"	22.12.15		Visited the 1st Aid Veterinary Station, and Mobile Veterinary Section, CHELMSFORD	A.P.
"	23.12.15		Inspected mange cases at BROWNINGS, and INGATESTONE, with Col. WALTERS, A.D.V.S., 3rd Army.	A.P.
"	24.12.15		Nil	A.P.
"	25.12.15		Nil	A.P.
"	26.12.15		Nil	A.P.
"	27.12.15		Nil	A.P.
"	28.12.15		Posted Lieut. T. BATTY, A.V.C., to the A.S.C., and 184th Inf. Bde., CHELMSFORD	A.P.

Army Form C. 2118.

WAR DIARY
OF A.D.V.S 61st (S.M.) DIVISION
INTELLIGENCE SUMMARY.

(Erase heading not required.)

Page 3.

Instructions regarding War Diaries and Intelligence Summaries are contained in F. S. Regs., Part II. and the Staff Manual respectively. Title pages will be prepared in manuscript.

Place	Date	Hour	Summary of Events and Information	Remarks and references to Appendices
BOREHAM.	29.12.15		Inspected horses at STOCK.	C.P.
"	30.12.15		Inspected sick horses at INGATESTONE.	C.P.
"	31.12.15		Interviewed Mr A.H. BROOKS, C.V.S., at MALDON., 3rd Army instructions.	C.P.

Arnold Pratt
MAJOR,
A.D.V.S. 61st (SOUTH MIDLAND) DIVISION.

CONFIDENTIAL

WAR DIARY OF

A.D.V.S. 61ST (SOUTH MIDLAND) DIVISION

FROM 1ST JANUARY, 1916, TO 31ST JANUARY, 1916.

VOLUME 2.

WAR DIARY
or
INTELLIGENCE SUMMARY.

Army Form C. 2118.

A.D.V.S 61st (S.M.) DIVISION.

(Erase heading not required.)

Place	Date	Hour	Summary of Events and Information	Remarks and references to Appendices
BOREHAM.	1-1-16		Nil	G.P.
"	2-1-16		Inspected horses at the 1st Aid Veterinary Station CHELMSFORD.	G.P.
"	3-1-16		Inspected sick horses of the 2/1st Brigade R.F.A., INGATESTONE.	A.P.
"	4-1-16		Inspected horses at GALLEYWOOD.	G.P.
"	5-1-16		Went to INGATESTONE, and BRENTWOOD, to inspect horses for casting.	Q.P.
"	6-1-16		Inspected sick horses at BROWNINGS, and INGATESTONE, with D.D.V.S, Central Force.	G.P.
"	7-1-16		Attended, Sale of horses at CHELMSFORD.	G.P.
"	8-1-16		Nil.	A.P.
"	9-1-16		Nil.	A.P.
"	10-1-16		Inspected horses at GREAT BADDOW.	Q.P.
"	11-1-16		Inspected horses of the 2/3rd Brigade, R.F.A., GREAT BADDOW.	A.P.
"	12-1-16		Inspected horses of the A.S.C. CHELMSFORD.	A.P.
"	13-1-16		Inspected horses of the 2/1st West Somerset Yeomanry, at LEXDEN.	A.P.
"	14-1-16		Visited the Mobile Veterinary Section, and Sick horses at CHELMSFORD.	A.P.
"	15-1-16		Inspected horses at SOUTHMINSTER, and MALDON.	A.P.
"	16-1-16		Nil.	A.P.

Army Form C. 2118.

WAR DIARY
or
INTELLIGENCE SUMMARY.
(Erase heading not required.)

A.D.V.S. 61st (S.M.) DIVISION

Page 2

Place	Date	Hour	Summary of Events and Information	Remarks and references to Appendices
BOREHAM.	17.1.16		Nil	A.P.
"	18.1.16		Went to DANBURY to inspect horses for casting.	A.P.
"	19.1.16		Inspected horses of the A.S.C., CHELMSFORD.	A.P.
"	20.1.16		Inspected horses at GREAT BADDOW.	A.P.
"	21.1.16		Inspected horses at the Mobile Veterinary Station.	A.P.
"	22.1.16		Went to BRENTWOOD to inspect horses for casting.	A.P.
"	23.1.16		Nil	A.P.
"	24.1.16		Inspected horses for casting belonging to the 31st R.F.A., INGATESTONE.	A.P.
"	25.1.16		Nil.	A.P.
"	26.1.16		Visited Mange Station, to inspect sick horses.	A.P.
"	27.1.16		Inspected horses for casting at BRENTWOOD.	A.P.
"	28.1.16		Went to COLCHESTER, and CLACTON-ON-SEA, to inspect horses.	A.P.
"	29.1.16		Nil.	A.P.
"	30.1.16		Went to SOUTHMINSTER, to inspect two horses left by the 8th Devon. Bde.	A.P.
"	31.1.16		Went to ELSENHAM and BUNTINGFORD, to inspect horses.	A.P.

Arnold Pruitt
MAJOR,
A.D.V.S., 61st (SOUTH MIDLAND) DIVISION

Confidential   Army Form C. 2118.

WAR DIARY
or
INTELLIGENCE SUMMARY.
(Erase heading not required.)

May 16
Vol. 19

Place	Date	Hour	Summary of Events and Information	Remarks and references to Appendices
Havre	23/5/16		Disembarked marched to No. 2. Rest Camp with Divisional Head Quarters	ACJ
"	24/5/16		Marched out of No. 2 Rest Camp, Entrained Horses of Divisional Head Quarters	ACJ
St Venant	25/5/16		Arrived St Venant.	ACJ
"	26/5/16		Office work. Inspected Head Quarters Horses Attd Head Quarters Signal Co.	ACJ
"	26/5/16		Office work. Inspected Head Quarters Horses	ACJ
"	27/5/16		Office work. Examined Head Quarters Horses & Signal Co.	ACJ
"	28/5/16		Office work. Examined Head Quarters Horses. Visited Mobile Veterinary Section.	ACJ
"	29/5/16		Office work. Examined Head Quarters Horses. Visited Mobile Veterinary Section. Interviews with A.D.V.S.	ACJ
"	30/5/16		Office work. Visited Examined Head Quarters Horses	ACJ
"	31/5/16		Office work - Examined Head Quarters Horses. Visited 1/10 Infantry Bde. Mobile Vety. Section	ACJ

A.C. Jones
Major A.V.C.

Army Form C. 2118.

WAR DIARY
or
INTELLIGENCE SUMMARY.
(Erase heading not required.)

Place	Date	Hour	Summary of Events and Information	Remarks and references to Appendices
S. Front	1/6/16		Office work. Visited Head Quarters Horses, Head Quarter Squad. C. Scammell, numerous Horses cadmed generally on Mange, Quers & the Line.	JRCT
"	2/6/16		Office work. Visited 61 Bde DAC + 306 Bde R.F.A also 182 Bde R.F.A. I note a number of animals of this Division were pulled down in Condition with their passing over, especially those that spent one day in Rest Camp. i.e marches into Rest Camp one afternoon, slept the next, the morning from the Town I have to Rest Camp being a fair march particularly all up hill this being especially severe on transport.	JRCT
"	3/6/16		Office work. Inspected Horses of Div Head Quarters.	JRCT
"	4/6/16		Office work. Sc Head Quarters (SOS) Horses. Visited Army Head Quarters, interview with D.D.V.S.	JRCT
"	5/6/16		Office work. Visited Head Quarter Signal Co, Sc Horses of Div Head Quarters	JRCT
"	6/6/16		Office work. Allowed Animals Div Head Quarters. Visited M.V.S.	JRCT
"	7/6/16		Office work. Sc H.Q. Animals - Visited Signal C. H.Q & 61. Div Train.	JRCT
"	8/6/16		Office work	JRCT
"	9/6/16		Office work.	JRCT

WAR DIARY
or
INTELLIGENCE SUMMARY.
(Erase heading not required.)

Army Form C. 2118.

Place	Date	Hour	Summary of Events and Information	Remarks and references to Appendices
St. Venant	10/6/16		Office work. Inspected 1st Head Quarters annuals	H.C.J
"	11/6/16		Office work.	H.C.J
"	12/6/16		Marched out & arrived La GORGE.	H.C.J
LA GORGE	13/6/16		Office work. Inspected Head Quarters Horses.	H.C.J
"	14/6/16		Office work. Visited 61. MOB. VET. SEC.	H.C.J
"	15/6/16		Office work. Inspected several Batteries of R.F.A. annuals looking well. Shoeing improving generally	H.C.J
"	16/6/16		Office work. Interviewed all Veterinary Officers of the division reference on the Vety. work of the division generally	H.C.J
"	17/6/16		Office. Inspected Horse Drawn stores.	H.C.J
"	18/6/16		Office work. Inspected Head Quarters Horses. reSalem of D.A.C.	H.C.J
"	19/6/16		Visited 184 Inf Bde. Head Quarters signals. Office work.	H.C.J
"	20/6/16		Office work.	H.C.J
"	21/6/16		Office. Head Quarters Signal Co. to inspect Horses.	H.C.J
"	22/6/16		Office work. Visited No:1 Co. Div Train	H.C.J
"	23/6/16		Office Work – Interviewed all Veterinary Officers re their work	H.C.J

WAR DIARY or INTELLIGENCE SUMMARY

Army Form C. 2118.

Place	Date	Hour	Summary of Events and Information	Remarks and references to Appendices
LA GORGE	24/6/16		Office work. Visited several units - Inspected animals, also Mobile Vety Sec & Dis Train	ACJ
"	25/6/16		- to inspect watering arrangements.	ACJ
"	25/6/16		Office work. Inspected H.Q. Horses	ACJ
"	26/6/16		Office work. Inspected H.Q. Signals	
"	27/6/16		Office work. Visited several Batteries Inspected Animals Enquired into watering & feeding arrangements, also shoeing	ACJ
"	28/6/16		Office work. Inspected more Artillery	ACJ
"	29/6/16		Office work. Corps accompanied the D.D.V.S. Inspecting Animals of the division.	ACJ
"	30/6/16		Finished the Inspection of Animals of the division. D.D.V.S. Expressed himself as satisfied with what he had seen.	ACJ

A.C. Jones.
Major A.V.C.
A.D.V.S. 61st Division.

WAR DIARY
or
INTELLIGENCE SUMMARY.

(Erase heading not required.)

Army Form C. 2118.

Place	Date	Hour	Summary of Events and Information	Remarks and references to Appendices
LA GORGE	1/7/16		Office work. Visited 305 Bde R.F.A. also Mobile Section	A.C.J.
"	2/7/16		Office work morning - attended Conference of D.D.V.S. afternoon	A.C.J.
"	3/7/16		" " Visited Corral units	J.C.J
"	4/7/16		Office work. Visited several units - inspected horses. 305 Bde. R.F.A.	A.C.J
"	5/7/16		Office. Isolated Horse Quarter Horses sent men.	A.C.J
"	6/7/16		Office. Inspected Horse Quarter Horses	A.C.J
"	7/7/16		Office. Inspected Horse Quarter Horses	A.C.J
"	8/7/16		Office. Inspected Corral Units & Horse Lines	A.C.J
"	9/7/16		Office. do do do	A.C.J
"	10/7/16		Office. Inspected Mobile Vety Sec. Horses under treatment &	A.C.J
"	11/7/16		Office. do do do	A.C.J
"	12/7/16		Office. Examined H.Q. Horses.	A.C.J
"	13/7/16		Office. arranged with Vety Officers their duties i case of an advance	A.C.J
"	14/7/16		Office. — do do do	A.C.J
"	15/7/16		Office. Visited H.Q. Horses.	A.C.J
"	16/7/16		Office. do do do	A.C.J.

Confidential

Army Form C. 2118.

Instructions regarding War Diaries and Intelligence Summaries are contained in F.S. Regs., Part II. and the Staff Manual respectively. Title pages will be prepared in manuscript.

WAR DIARY
or
INTELLIGENCE SUMMARY.
(Erase heading not required.)

Place	Date	Hour	Summary of Events and Information	Remarks and references to Appendices
LA GORGUE.	17/7/16		Office work. Inspected mobile Sec^n stores.	A.D.V.S
"	18/7/16		Office. Visited units	A.D.V.S
"	19/7/16		Office. Inspected mobile Sec^n stores for trenches	A.D.V.S
"	20/7/16		Office work.	A.D.V.S
"	21/7/16		Office work. Inspected Heavy Quarter horses.	A.D.V.S
"	22/7/16		Office work. Visited R.F.A. Bde.	A.D.V.S
"	23/7/16		Office work. Visited H^d Q^rs horses. Mobile Vet^y Section	A.D.V.S
"	24/7/16		Office work. " " "	A.D.V.S
"	25/7/16		Office. Visited H^d Q Horses.	A.D.V.S
"	26/7/16		Office. Visited Divisional units	A.D.V.S
"	27/7/16		Office " " "	A.D.V.S
"	28/7/16		Office. Visited R.F.A. Bde.	A.D.V.S
"	29/7/16		Office " " "	A.D.V.S
"	30/7/16		Office " " "	A.D.V.S
"	31/7/16		Office. Visited 308 Bde. R.F.A.	A.D.V.S

During the month I have visited the animals of this Division. I find the transport good. also D.A.C. & Train. R.F.A. have improved animals.

J.L.C. Joyce Major. A.D.V.S. 61st Div.

WAR DIARY or INTELLIGENCE SUMMARY

Army Form C. 2118.

Place	Date	Hour	Summary of Events and Information	Remarks and references to Appendices
LA GORGUE	1/8/16		Office work. Visited 1st Labour Batt. R.E. & C.R.A. Examined Divisional Hd Quarters Animals.	A.D.C.J.
"	2/8/16		Office work. Visited C.R.A. Div Head Quarters Wagons &c. also 61st Div Train Farriers Horses.	A.D.C.J.
"	3/8/16		Office work. Visited Reserve Horses at Head Quarters Div R.E.A.	A.D.C.J.
"	4/8/16		Office work. Visited C. Batt. 306 Bde R.F.A. 1st & 2nd M.V.S. afternoon Conference with Veterinary Officers of the Division	A.D.C.J.
"	—			
"	5/8/16		Office work. Inspected Div Head Quarters Horses.	A.D.C.J.
"	6/8/16		Attended Conference at Office of D.D.V.S. 1st Army.	A.D.C.J.
"	7/8/16		Office — Inspected Animals of the 305 & 306 Bde R.F.A.	A.D.C.J.
"	8/8/16		Office. Visited Div Head Quarters Animals also M.V.S. & 2/1st D.A.C.	A.D.C.J.
"	9/8/16		Office — Visited Div Head Quarters Animals	A.D.C.J.
"	10/8/16		Office — Visited 182 Inf Bde, Sgl. Field Co R.E.	A.D.C.J.
"	11/8/16		Office — Conference with Veterinary Officers of the Division	A.D.C.J.
"	12/8/16		Office. Inspected Reserve mules also animals of D. Batt. 306 Bde R.F.A.	A.D.C.J.
"	13/8/16		Office. Visited 61st M.V.S. The G.O.C. Division was there expressed very Satisfaction with the Section, also the DAQMG who saw all animals in the Section	A.D.C.J.
"	14/8/16		Office — Visited D.H.Q. Inspected Animals of B/304 & D/305 R.F.A.	A.D.C.J.

Confidential

Army Form C. 2118.

WAR DIARY
or
INTELLIGENCE SUMMARY.

(Erase heading not required.)

Instructions regarding War Diaries and Intelligence Summaries are contained in F. S. Regs., Part II. and the Staff Manual respectively. Title pages will be prepared in manuscript.

Place	Date	Hour	Summary of Events and Information	Remarks and references to Appendices
LA GORGUE	15/9/16		Office - Visited 163rd Inf Bde Horse Ammunition Their Quarters	A.D.V.S.
"	16/9/16		Office - J arrivals Div Head Quarters	A.D.V.S.
"	17/9/16		Office - Visited Horse Ammunition arrivals of C. Rds 305 R.T.R. N°.1 Co. A.S.C. & M.V.S.	A.D.V.S.
"	18/9/16		Office - Visited Head Quarters C.R.A. 183 Inf Bde, M.V.S. afternoon Conference with	A.D.V.S.
"			Veterinary Officers of the Division	
"	19/8/16		Office - See arrivals of Div Head Quarters	A.D.V.S.
"	20/9/16		Office - Visited M.V.S.	A.D.V.S.
"	21/9/16		Office - Visited 184 Inf Bde & 308 Bde R.T.R.	A.D.V.S.
"	22/9/16		Office - Visited H.Q. Signals & M.V.S.	A.D.V.S.
"	23/9/16		Office - Visited H.Q. Signal Co. & M.V.S.	A.D.V.S.
"	24/9/16		Office - Visited Horse Ammunition its H.Q. arrivals Signals Co.	A.D.V.S.
"	25/9/16		Office - Visited Horses on H.Q. arrivals Signals Co.	A.D.V.S.
"	26/9/16		Office - Visited M.V.S. Div H.Q. & 163 Machine Gun Co.	A.D.V.S.
"	27/9/16		Office - Visited 308 Bde R.T.R. H.Q. Signal Co.	A.D.V.S.
"	28/9/16		Visited three Veterinary Hospitals in Lines of Communication to by horse	A.D.V.S.
"			of D.D.V.S. 1st Army -	

Confidential

WAR DIARY
or
INTELLIGENCE SUMMARY

Army Form C. 2118.

Place	Date	Hour	Summary of Events and Information	Remarks and references to Appendices
A. GORGUE	29/7/16		Offrs:- Initia tois 1st R animals also M.M.P. Regmts C.	H.C.J
"	30/7/16		Offrs: inort. initia D.H.Q + C.R.A.	H.C.J
"	31/7/16		Offrs: initia D.H.Q + D Batt 307 Bde R.F.A.	H.C.J
			The animals of the R.F.A. are improving in condition especially during this month showing in improving hair also been much to be desired, it is receiving special attention under supervision of the V.Os. — During the month the dosing of the Division with mallein by the Palpebral method has been completed, 8 animals reacted more distinctly, but no two reaminations confirmed the result of the test, fortunately no suspects were not applied in these cases. The Palpebral method is a great advance on the Sub-cutaneous method as it appears to be quite as accurate & does not require that the animals to be should go off duty —	H.C.J
			H.C.Jones Major A.D.V.S. 61st Division.	

A.D.V.S.
No.
Date 29/8/16
61st (S.M.) DIV.

Confidential

Army Form C. 2118.

WAR DIARY
or
INTELLIGENCE SUMMARY
(Erase heading not required.)

Instructions regarding War Diaries and Intelligence Summaries are contained in F.S. Regs., Part II. and the Staff Manual respectively. Title pages will be prepared in manuscript.

Vol 5

Place	Date	Hour	Summary of Events and Information	Remarks and references to Appendices
LA GORGUE	1/9/16	Office	Arr. R.T.O.	ADS J
"	2/9/16	Office	do - do -	ADS J
"	3/9/16	Office	Visited Mobile Veterinary Section ~ Conference J.D.D.V.S. 1st Army.	ADS J
"	4/9/16	Office	Visited Mobile Veterinary Section - Inspected Animals for Evacuation	ADS J
"	5/9/16	Office	Visited N° 4 Sec. DAC. & 305 Ary Bde.	ADS J
"	6/9/16	Office	Visited Inspected Animals D.H.Q. Signals Co & C.R.A. also 3rd Field Ambce.	ADS J
"	7/9/16	Office	Visited 3rd Field Ambulance - DHQ - M.M.P. - Mobile Section	ADS J
"	8/9/16	Office	Visited C.R.A, & C.R.E. Inspected Animals & Mules &c.	ADS J
"	9/9/16	Office	Visited D.H.Q. - Train Quarter Signal Co.	ADS J
"	10/9/16	Office	Visited DHQ Mobile Veterinary Section - Inspected all Animals.	ADS J
"	11/9/16	Office	Visited N° 4 Base Veterinary Hospital.	ADS J
"	12/9/16	Office		ADS J
"	13/9/16	Office	Visited DHQ, & C.R.E. Inspected Animals 163 Ary Bde.	ADS J
"	14/9/16	Office	Visited 305 Bde R.F.A. 306 Bde R.F.A. + H.Qs 163 Ary Bde.	ADS J
"	15/9/16	Office	Visited 306 Bde R.F.A. Inspected all Animals	ADS J
"	16/9/16	Office	Inspected Animals 162 Ary Bde & 3/1 Field C.R.E.	ADS J

Army Form C. 2118.

WAR DIARY
or
INTELLIGENCE SUMMARY.
(Erase heading not required.)

Instructions regarding War Diaries and Intelligence Summaries are contained in F. S. Regs., Part II. and the Staff Manual respectively. Title pages will be prepared in manuscript.

Confidential

Place	Date	Hour	Summary of Events and Information	Remarks and references to Appendices
LA GORGUE	17/9/16		Office. Visited 306 Bde R.F.A. a H.Q. 184 dry Bde.	ADCJ
"	18/9/16		Office. Visited D.H.Q. & Artric M. See. Inspected Animals	ADCJ
"	19/9/16		Office. Visited D.H.Q. a No.2 Sec. D.A.C.	ADCJ
"	20/9/16		Office. Visited D.H.Q. a 2/2 Field Ambulance	ADCJ
"	21/9/16		Office. Visited D.H.Q. & Signal C. Inspected Animals	ADCJ
"	22/9/16		Office. Visited D.H.Q. a 2/3 Field Ambulance - Inspected animals	ADCJ
"	23/9/16		Office. Visited No.1 Sec. D.A.C. & 304 Bde R.F.A.	ADCJ
"	24/9/16		Office. Visited No.3 Co. A.S.C. D.H.Q. No.2 Co. A.S.C. with D.D.R. & Surplus Horses.	ADCJ
"	25/9/16		Office. Visited No. 2 Sec. D.A.C.	ADCJ
"	26/9/16		Office. Visited No.1 Co. A.S.C. 173 Batt. 304 Bde R.F.A.	ADCJ
"	27/9/16		Office. Visited D.H.Q. & H.Q. Signal C.	ADCJ
"	28/9/16		Office. Visited A Batt. 304 Bde R.F.A.	ADCJ
"	29/9/16		Office. D.H.Q. & H.Q. Signal C. Inspected animals	ADCJ
"	30/9/16		Office. D.H.Q. & H.Q. Signal C. also M.M.P. Inspected animals.	ADCJ
			The animals of the Division are improving generally, there is a marked improvement in R.F.A. during the month.	

A.C. Jones
Major A.V.C.

Army Form C. 2118.

WAR DIARY
or
INTELLIGENCE SUMMARY.
(Erase heading not required.)

Place	Date	Hour	Summary of Events and Information	Remarks and references to Appendices
LA GORGUE	1/10/16	Office	Visited Mobile Veterinary Sectn. Inspected all animals.	A.C.T.
-	2/10/16	Office.	"	A.C.T.
"	3/10/16	Office.	Inspected Head Quarters Animals of the division.	A.C.T.
"	4/10/16	Office.	Proceeded to England on 10 days leave, however on duties of A.D.V.S. — Capt. Reed A.V.C. will act in my absence	A.C.T.
	5/10/16	Office.	Visited 1, 2, 3, 4 Cos A.P.C.	Asst R
	6/10/16	Office.	Inspections Remounts, Vet. Hos. Sig. C. 2/6 Glos. R. 2/7 Hos. R. 2/7 M.E.B.	Asst R
	7/10/16	Office.	Visited Divn. trains.	Asst R
	8/10/16	Office.	Visited Div. Stres Zunners, 3 Co. A.S.C. 2/6 Gloster Regt.	Asst R
	9/10/16	Office.	Visited Mobile Veterinary Sectn. Divl Hres. Zunners.	Asst R
	10/10/16	Office	Visited Mobile Veterinarian Sectn. 183 Inf. Bde.	Asst R
	11/10/16	Office	Visited D.H.Q. C.R.A. Hd 2, 3, 4 Co. A.S.C.	Asst R
	12/10/16	Office	Visited D.H.Q. Signal C. R.E. 1 Co. A.S.C.	Asst R
	13/10/16	Office	Visited D.H.Q. Signal C R.E. 183 Inf. Bde.	Asst R
	14/10/16	Office	Visited Divl. Train. Signal C. R.E.	Asst R
	15/10/16	Office	Visited 183 Inf. Bde. 2, 3, 4 Co. A.S.C. Signal C.R.E. D.H.Q.	Asst R

Confidential

Army Form C. 2118.

WAR DIARY
or
INTELLIGENCE SUMMARY.
(Erase heading not required.)

Instructions regarding War Diaries and Intelligence Summaries are contained in F.S. Regs., Part II. and the Staff Manual respectively. Title pages will be prepared in manuscript.

Place	Date	Hour	Summary of Events and Information	Remarks and references to Appendices
LA GORGUE	15/10/16		Returned to duty from 10 days leave. Roots over from Capt. Reid A.V.C.	A.C.J.
"	16/10/16		Office. Visited D.H.Q. Inspected all animals also C.R.A.	A.C.J.
"	17/10/16		Office. Visited Mobile Veterinary Sec. & 307 Bde R.F.A.	A.C.J.
"	18/10/16		Office. Attended Inspection at D.H.Q.	A.C.J.
"	19/10/16		Office. Inspected animals of 3rd Bde R.F.A. Visited Head Quarters 182 Bde Inf. Bde.	A.C.J.
"	20/10/16		Office. Visited 306 Bde R.F.A. Conference afternoon with D.Os. of the Division	A.C.J.
"	21/10/16		Office. Inspected 31. Reinforcements. Visited H.Q. Signals Co. Horses Issued Reinforcements	A.C.J.
"	22/10/16		Office.	A.C.J.
"	23/10/16		Office. Visited Mobile Sec. No. 1 Co. on train Inspected Reinforcements	A.C.J.
"	24/10/16		Office. Visited C.R.A. H.Q. Signals Co.	A.C.J.
"	25/10/16		Office. Visited Mobile Sec.	A.C.J.
"	26/10/16		Office.	A.C.J.
"	27/10/16		Office. Conference of Veterinary Officers afternoon	A.C.J.
ST. VENANT	28/10/16		Travelled to with Div H.Qrs.	A.C.J.
"	29/10/16		Office. Visited 61st DAC with DAQMG. Examined animals	A.C.J.
"	30/10/16		Office. Visited Div H.Q. animals – Signals Co. & M.M.P. also 61st Mot. D. Sec.	A.C.J.

Confidential

Army Form C. 2118.

WAR DIARY
or
INTELLIGENCE SUMMARY.

(Erase heading not required.)

Instructions regarding War Diaries and Intelligence Summaries are contained in F. S. Regs., Part II. and the Staff Manual respectively. Title pages will be prepared in manuscript.

Place	Date	Hour	Summary of Events and Information	Remarks and references to Appendices
ST. VENANT.	31/10/16		Office - Visits to H.Q. animals & mobile Veterinary Section.	A.D.C.S.

H.C. Jones
Major.

Confidential

Army Form C. 2118.

WAR DIARY
or
INTELLIGENCE SUMMARY.
(Erase heading not required.)

Instructions regarding War Diaries and Intelligence Summaries are contained in F. S. Regs., Part II. and the Staff Manual respectively. Title pages will be prepared in manuscript.

A.D.V.S.
No. —
Date 1/11/16.
61st (S.M.) DIVISION

Vol 7

Place	Date	Hour	Summary of Events and Information	Remarks and references to Appendices
ST. VENANT	1/11/16		Office. Ex Div H.Q. arrived & Signal Co.	A.C.J.
"	2/11/16		Marched out of ST. VENANT, arrive CHELERS. 2.p.m.	J.E.C.J
CHELERS.	3/11/16		Office. See also annual Divisional H.Q.	A.C.J
"	4/11/16		Marched out of CHELERS. 10 a.m. with D.H.Q. arrive ROELLECOURT. 12 noon.	A.C.J.
ROELLECOURT	5/11/16		Office	A.C.J
"	6/11/16		Marched out of ROELLECOURT. 10 a.m. arr. FROHEN-LE-GRAND. 2.p.m.	A.C.J
FROHEN-LE-GRAND	7/11/16		Office. re annual of D.H.Q.	A.C.J
"	8/11/16		Office. Co. annual of D.H.Q	A.C.J
"	9/11/16		Office	A.C.J
"	10/11/16		Office. Inspected 61st MOB. VET. SEC. & No.2 Co A.S.C. Examined 6 Returns—	A.C.J
"	11/11/16		Office. Visits 184 Inf Bde. Exam. ST. LAINE of Nob Vet Sec. Sent to A.C.S. Ill.	A.C.J
"	12/11/16		Office. Visits Nob Vet. Sec. Exam. Q. W. REID approved temporary for below.	A.C.J
"	13/11/16		Office. Visits D.H.Q arrival of Belgian attaches —	A.C.J
"	14/11/16		Office. Visits D.H.Q. arrival & No.4 Co A.S.C.	A.C.J
BERNAVILLE	15/11/16		Marched from FROHEN-LE-GRAND to BERNAVILLE	A.C.J
"	16/11/16		Office.	A.C.J.

Confidential

Army Form C. 2118.

WAR DIARY
or
INTELLIGENCE SUMMARY.
(Erase heading not required.)

Instructions regarding War Diaries and Intelligence Summaries are contained in F. S. Regs. Part II. and the Staff Manual respectively. Title pages will be prepared in manuscript.

Place	Date	Hour	Summary of Events and Information	Remarks and references to Appendices
BERNAVILLE.	16/11/16		Marched out & arrived CANAPLES. Saw as many animals as possible on the march.	A.D.C.J
CANAPLES.	17/11/16		Marched out from CANAPLES & arrived CONTAY. 1 p.m.	A.D.C.J
CONTAY.	18/11/16		Office. Inspected animals 188 Bde Bde. Visited by D.D.V.S. 5th Army.	A.D.C.J
"	19/11/16		Office. Visited 61st MOB. VET. SEC.	A.D.C.J
"	20/11/16		Office. Visited H.Q. Signal Co. & Mob. Vet Sec.	A.D.C.J
"	21/11/16		Office. Visited A.D.V.S. 1st DIV. re taking over from him Mobile Section	A.D.C.J
"	22/11/16		Marched out & arrived BOUZINCOURT.	A.D.C.J
BOUZINCOURT.	23/11/16		Office.	A.D.C.J
"	24/11/16		Office.	A.D.C.J
"	25/11/16		Office - Inspected 306 Bde R.F.A. animals & Billets for 61st Mot. Vet. Sec.	A.D.C.J
"	26/11/16		Office. " Divisional Train A.S.C.	A.D.C.J
"	27/11/16		Office. Inspected Div. H.Q. & animals.	A.D.C.J
"	28/11/16		Office - Five Shells into the Camp. 2 Horses 18th Div. C.R.A. Killed	A.D.C.J
"	29/11/16		Office. Inspected H.Q. & animals	A.D.C.J
"	30/11/16		Office - Conference F.O.E. 61st & 18th Div. R.F.A.	A.D.C.J

F.C. Ames.
Major.
A.D.V.S. 61st Div.

Confidential

Army Form C. 2118.

WAR DIARY
or
INTELLIGENCE SUMMARY.
(Erase heading not required.)

Vol 8

Place	Date	Hour	Summary of Events and Information	Remarks and references to Appendices
BOUZINCOURT	1/12/16		Office. Inspected Div H.Q. animals	ADVS
"	2/12/16		Office. Visited MOB.VET-SEC. 304 & 305 Bdes R.F.A	ADVS
"	3/12/16		Office. Inspected Div H.Q. animals.	ADVS
"	4/12/16		Office. Visited 61st D.A.C. Inspected animals	ADVS
"	5/12/16		Office – Sc D.H.Q. animals	ADVS
"	6/12/16		Office – Sc D.H.Q. animals – Camp Shelled. No animals injured	ADVS
"	7/12/16		Office. Sc D.H.Q. animals – Visited C.R.A. Sc animals	ADVS
"	8/12/16		Office. Sc D.H.Q. Horses. Conference with V.Os. of Division	ADVS
"	9/12/16		Office. Sc D.H.Q. Horses.	ADVS
"	10/12/16		Office.	ADVS
"	11/12/16		Office. Visited 304 & 305 Bde R.F.A. also Mobile Veterinary Section.	ADVS
"	12/12/16		Office. Visited N°.1 Co Train A.S.C.	ADVS
"	13/12/16		Office. Visited N°.1 Co Train A.S.C. & 304 Bde R.F.A. Inspected 46. Runners	ADVS
"	14/12/16		Office. Gathered Quarter animals. Visited 304 Bde R.F.A.	ADVS
"	15/12/16		Office. Conference with V.Os. of the Division.	ADVS
"	16/12/16		Office	ADVS

Confidential

Army Form C. 2118.

WAR DIARY
or
INTELLIGENCE SUMMARY.
(Erase heading not required.)

Instructions regarding War Diaries and Intelligence Summaries are contained in F.S. Regs., Part II. and the Staff Manual respectively. Title pages will be prepared in manuscript.

A.D.V.S. No. Date 17/12/16 61st (S.M.) DIVISION

Place	Date	Hour	Summary of Events and Information	Remarks and references to Appendices
BOUZINCOURT	19/12/16	Office	Head Quarters Arrivals	JFCJ
"	18/12/16	Office	"	JFCJ
"	19/12/16	Office	"	JFCJ
"	20/12/16	Office	Co. Head Quarters Arrivals	JFCJ
"	21/12/16	Office	"	JFCJ
"	22/12/16	Office	Visited 61st Div Train A.S.C. & 162 Inf Bde	JFCJ
"	23/12/16	Office	"	JFCJ
"	24/12/16	Office	Visited 306 Art. Bde.	JFCJ
"	25/12/16	Office	Sc. Hd. Q. arrivals	JFCJ
"	26/12/16	Office	Visited 164 Machine Gun Co. Mobile Vety Sec	JFCJ
"	27/12/16	Office	& arrivals D.H.Q.	JFCJ
"	28/12/16	Office	Visited Army Hd. Q. Conference at Office D.D.V.S. Army	JFCJ
"	29/12/16	Office	Co. arrivals at D.H.Q.	JFCJ
"	30/12/16	Office		JFCJ
"	31/12/16	Office		JFCJ

I have frequently inspected arrivals of the Division during the past month. Hard standing are urgently required & are specially trying conditions require to be improved owing to new Essilunia of camps.

J. C. Jones Major.
A.D.V.S. 61st Div.

Confidential

Army Form C. 2118.

WAR DIARY
or
INTELLIGENCE SUMMARY.
(Erase heading not required.)

Instructions regarding War Diaries and Intelligence Summaries are contained in F. S. Regs., Part II. and the Staff Manual respectively. Title pages will be prepared in manuscript.

Vol 9

Place	Date	Hour	Summary of Events and Information	Remarks and references to Appendices
BOUZINCOURT	1/1/19	Office	Inspected animals of 156 Bde R.F.A.	ALCJ
"	2/1/19	Office		ALCJ
"	3/1/19	Office	Inspected Hd Q. Horses	ALCJ
"	4/1/19	Office	ditto	ALCJ
"	5/1/19	Office	Visited 61st D.A.C	ALCJ
"	6/1/19	Office	Visited 61st D.A.C	ALCJ
"	7/1/19	Office	Inspected all watering arrangements of the Division	ALCJ
"	8/1/19	Office	Inspected Animals Hd Q.C. Signals	ALCJ
"	9/1/19	Office	Visited Motor Vet: Sec. Inspected animals 307 Bde R.F.A.	ALCJ
"	10/1/19	Office	See Hd Q animals of the Division	ALCJ
"	11/1/19	Office	See watering troughs of the Division & Company Hd DAQMG.	ALCJ
"	12/1/19	Office	G Hd Q Signals Co' animals. Visited Div Train A.S.C.	ALCJ
"	13/1/19	Office	Ex Remounts.	JLCJ
"	14/1/19	Office		JLCJ
"	15/1/19	Office	Visited C.R.A. 9 animals	JLCJ
"	16/1/19		Marched out of BOUZINCOURT to MARIEUX.	JLCJ

Confidential

Army Form C. 2118.

Instructions regarding War Diaries and Intelligence Summaries are contained in F. S. Regs., Part II. and the Staff Manual respectively. Title pages will be prepared in manuscript.

WAR DIARY
or
INTELLIGENCE SUMMARY.
(Erase heading not required.)

Place	Date	Hour	Summary of Events and Information	Remarks and references to Appendices
MARIEUX.	17/1/17.		Marched from MARIEUX to BERNAVILLE. Garrison guards of the infantry Luny ort. also trains (A.S.C) arrived at the trench.	A.C.J.
"	18/1/17.		Office. G. bis H.Q. arrival.	A.C.J.
BERNAVILLE.	19/1/17.		Marched from BERNAVILLE to BRAILLY.	A.C.J.
"	20/1/17.		Office. & D.H.Q. arrivals.	A.C.J.
BRAILLY.	21/1/17.		Office. Visited Mob. Vet. Sec. at NEUVILLE & 61st D.A.C. at MAIZICOURT.	A.C.J.
"	22/1/17.		Office. Visited 1/2 Highland Field A.R.E. at MARENEVILLE & 1/2 Scot. Raur. Horses	A.C.J.
"	23/1/17.		Office. Visited 1st Div H.Q. Arrivals. also M.M.P.	A.C.J.
"	24/1/17.		Office. Visited Arrivals D.H.Q.	A.C.J.
"	25/1/17.		Office. & arrivals 182 H.Q., 183 Q.C., The Q.C. Signals	A.C.J.
"	26/1/17.		Office. & Horses of M.M.P. Conference with Bug Officer	A.C.J.
"	27/1/17.		Office. & arrivals. 304 Bde 12 F.A. & one Batt. 308 Bde. also D.A.C.	A.C.J.
"	28/1/17.		Office. & arrivals 306 Bde R.F.A.	A.C.J.
"	29/1/17.		Office. Visited Mob. Vet. Sec. & 304 Bde R.F.A.	A.C.J.
"	30/1/17.		Office. Visited 61st D.A.C.	A.C.J.
"	31/1/17.		Office. Conference at D.H.Q. & Visited 306 & 304 Bde R.F.A.	J.L.C.J.

J.L.C. Jones. Major.
A.D.V.S. 61st Division.

WAR DIARY
or
INTELLIGENCE SUMMARY.
(Erase heading not required.)

Army Form C. 2118.

Confidential

Instructions regarding War Diaries and Intelligence Summaries are contained in F.S. Regs., Part II. and the Staff Manual respectively. Title pages will be prepared in manuscript.

A.D.V.S. 61st (S.M.) DIVISION
No. 1/2/17
Date 1/2/17

Vol 10

Place	Date	Hour	Summary of Events and Information	Remarks and references to Appendices
BRAILLY.	1/2/17		Office. Visited 184 Inf Bde at MAISON PONTHIEU.	ACJ
"	2/2/17		Office. do do do.	ACJ
"	3/2/17		Office. Visited Inspected Animals of 307 Bde R.F.A.	ACJ
"	4/2/17		Office. Inspected Animals of 306 Bde. R.F.A.	ACJ
"	5/2/17		Marched from BRAILLY to LONG.	ACJ
LONG.	6/2/17.		Office opened at LONG.	ACJ
"	7/2/17		Inspected 183 Inf Bde. & D.C.I. Visited O.C. MOB. VET. SEC.	ACJ
"	8/2/17		Office. Visited 61st D.A.C. at LONGPRÉ.	ACJ
"	9/2/17		Office. Interview with D.D.V.S. 4th Army.	ACJ
"	10/2/17		Office. Attended Conference at D.H.Q.	ACJ
"	11/2/17		Office. Visited 61st D.A.C. 306 & 307 Bds R.F.A. Inspected Animals for the March.	ACJ
"	12/2/17		Office. Inspected 306 Bde R.F.A. on the March.	ACJ
"	13/2/17		Inspected 307 Bde R.F.A. & 184 Inf Bde on the March.	ACJ
"	14/2/17		Rode from LONG. to GUILLAUCOURT.	ACJ
GUILLAUCOURT	15/2/17		Office. Inspected the Quarter Animals.	ACJ
"	16/2/17		Office.	ACJ

Confidential

Army Form C. 2118.

WAR DIARY
or
INTELLIGENCE SUMMARY.
(Erase heading not required.)

Instructions regarding War Diaries and Intelligence Summaries are contained in F. S. Regs., Part II. and the Staff Manual respectively. Title pages will be prepared in manuscript.

A.D.V.S.
No.
Date 17/2/17
61st (S.M.) DIV

Place	Date	Hour	Summary of Events and Information	Remarks and references to Appendices
GUILLAUCOURT.	17/2/17		Office. Inspected Hd Q. annexe 172 Q Signal C.	A.C.J
HARBOINNERS.	18/2/17		March from GUILLAUCOURT to HARBOINNERS.	A.C.J
"	19/2/17		Office opened.	A.C.J
"	20/2/17		Office. Visited Motor Vety Sec.	A.C.J
"	21/2/17		Office. Visited 306 Bde R.F.A.	A.C.J
"	22/2/17		Office. Visited D's Train. A.S.C. & 61st D.A.C.	A.C.J
"	23/2/17		Office. Visited 306 & 304 Bdes. R.F.A.	A.C.J
"	24/2/17		Office. Visited Mot Vet Sec. & 61st D.A.C.	A.C.J
"	25/2/17		Office. Visited Mot Vet Sec. & 61st D.A.C.	A.C.J
"	26/2/17		Office. Visited 61st D.A.C. & 306 Bde R.F.A.	A.C.J
"	27/2/17		Office. Visited Personnel annexe & Motor Veterinary Section.	A.C.J
"	28/2/17		Office. Autumn Conference D.D.V.S. 4th Army.	A.C.J

A.C.Jones.
Major.
A.D.V.S. 61st Division.

Army Form C. 2118.

WAR DIARY
or
INTELLIGENCE SUMMARY.
(Erase heading not required.)

Vol XI

Place	Date	Hour	Summary of Events and Information	Remarks and references to Appendices
HARBOINNERES	1/3/17		Office. - Visited 307 Bde R.F.A. also mobile Veterinary Section	ADCJ
"	2/3/17		Office. Conference C.O.s. Attended Inspection by G.O.C. of 306 & 307 Bdes. R.F.A.	ADCJ
"	3/3/17		Office. - Visited Recovered Animals & Mob. Vet. Sec.	ADCJ
"	4/3/17		Office. - See Hd Q. Animals	ADCJ
"	5/3/17		Office. - Visited Mob Vet Sec. & 61st D.A.C.	ADCJ
"	6/3/17		Office. - Visited Mob Vet Sec. Frozen Saddles Stores.	ADCJ
"	7/3/17		Office. - Visited Mob Vet Sec. & 61st Div Train A.S.C. Recovered Horses & Mules.	ADCJ
"	8/3/17		Office. - Visited Mob Vet Sec	ADCJ
"	9/3/17		Office. - Visited 61st D.A.C. & Div Train. A.S.C.	ADCJ
"	10/3/17		Office. - Visited D.H.Q. Animals & Mob Vet Sec.	ADCJ
"	11/3/17		Office. - Visited Mob Vet Sec. & M.M.P.	ADCJ
"	12/3/17		Office. - Visited 306 & 307 Bdes. R.F.A. 496. Field Co. R.E. & Mob Vet Sec.	ADCJ
"	13/3/17		Office. - Visited 61st D.A.C. Sick Lines. 3rd Field Ambulance. M.M.P. 61st Q. Signal Co.	ADCJ
"	14/3/17		Office. - Visited Sick Lines 61st D.A.C. also Mobile Veterinary Sec. Examined Animals for Evacuation.	ADCJ
"	15/3/17		Office. - Visited Recovered Animals 61st Q. Signal Co.	ADCJ

2353 Wt. W2544/1454 700,000 5/15 D. D. & L. A.D.S.S. Forms/C. 2118.

Confidential

Army Form C. 2118.

WAR DIARY
or
INTELLIGENCE SUMMARY.
(Erase heading not required.)

Instructions regarding War Diaries and Intelligence Summaries are contained in F. S. Regs., Part II. and the Staff Manual respectively. Title pages will be prepared in manuscript.

Place	Date	Hour	Summary of Events and Information	Remarks and references to Appendices
HARBOINNÈRES.	16/3/17		Office. Examined Animals D.H.Q. Visited 61st Mobile Veterinary Section.	ADVS
"	17/3/17		Office. Examined Horse in Mobile Vety Sec.	"
"	18/3/17		Office. Examined Animals at D.H.Q.	ADVS
	19/3/17		Office. Attended Conference, D.D.V.S at Army Hd Q.	ADVS
	20/3/17		Office. Visited 61st D.A.C.	ADVS
	21/3/17		Office - Went up the line, examined by Transport Animals at work	ADVS
	22/3/17		Office. D.H.Q animals. Visited Mob Vety Sec.	ADVS
	23/3/17		Office. Visited 306 Bde R.F.A. Conference with V.Os.	ADVS
	24/3/17		Office. D H Q animals. Mob Vet Sec	ADVS
	25/3/17		Office. Inspected animals in Mob Vet Sec to evacuation	ADVS
	26/3/17		Office. Visited 61st D.A.C.	ADVS
	27/3/17		Office. Visited & examined all Sick animals 61st D.A.C.	ADVS
	28/3/17		Office. Examined D.H.Q. animals. Visited 61st Mob Vet Sec.	ADVS
	29/3/17		Marched out of HARBOINNÈRES to GUIZANCOURT.	ADVS
GUIZANCOURT.	30/3/17		Office. Conference with Veterinary Officers	ADVS
"	31/3/17		Office. Visited 306 & 307 Bde R.F.A.	ADVS

J.C.C Jones Major
A.D.V.S. 61st Division

Army Form C. 2118.

WAR DIARY
or
INTELLIGENCE SUMMARY.
(Erase heading not required.)

Instructions regarding War Diaries and Intelligence Summaries are contained in F. S. Regs., Part II. and the Staff Manual respectively. Title pages will be prepared in manuscript.

Place	Date	Hour	Summary of Events and Information	Remarks and references to Appendices
GUIZANCOURT.	1/4/17.		Office. Visited 184 Inf. Bde. & Annual at D.H.Q	J.C.C.T.
"	2/4/17		Office. "	J.C.C.T.
"	3/4/17		Office. Daily M.M.P. Mobiles Vety. Sec.	J.C.C.T.
"	4/4/17		Office. Visited 183 Inf Bde	J.C.C.T.
"	5/4/17		Office. Visited DIV. TRAIN. with D.A.Q.M.G.	J.C.C.T.
"	6/4/17		Office. Visited Train. A.S.C. Inspected Horses	J.C.C.T.
"	7/4/17		Office. Visited D.H.Q. Annual & 110 H.BATTERY. Conference V.Os.	J.C.C.T.
"	8/4/17		Office. Visited 184 Inf Bde.	J.C.C.T.
"	9/4/17		Office. Visited 61st D.A.C.	J.C.C.T.
"	10/4/17		Office. Visited 61st Mot Ver Sec. & Annual	J.C.C.T.
"	11/4/17		Office. & D.H.Q. Annual	J.C.C.T.
"	12/4/17		Office. Visited 183 Inf Bde.	J.C.C.T.
"	13/4/17		Marched from GUIZANCOURT. to VOYENNES. Office. Inspected D.H.Q. Horses. M.M.P. Horses visited Mobile 4/6. G. R.E.	J.C.C.T.
VOYENNES.	14/4/17		Office. Attended Q Conference	J.C.C.T.
"	15/4/17		Office. Examined D.H.Q. Annual	J.C.C.T.
"	16/4/17.		Office. Visited Mob VCI- See Scanned Belec. Annual &c.	J.C.C.T

Confidential

Army Form C. 2118.

61st Division
19/4/17.

WAR DIARY
or
INTELLIGENCE SUMMARY.

(Erase heading not required.)

Instructions regarding War Diaries and Intelligence Summaries are contained in F. S. Regs., Part II. and the Staff Manual respectively. Title pages will be prepared in manuscript.

Place	Date	Hour	Summary of Events and Information	Remarks and references to Appendices
VOYENNES.	17/4/17		Office – Visits 164th Bde.	J.E.C.T.
"	18/4/17		Office. & Annuals D.H.Q. – Interview with A.D.V.S. 32nd Div.	A.C.T.
"	19/4/17		Office. Visits M.M.P. & Hd Q Signals Co. also Hd Vet Sec. 32nd Div as taking over	A.C.T.
"	20/4/17		Office. to D.H.Q. Annuals	A.C.J.
"	21/4/17		Office	A.C.J.
"	22/4/17		Moves out of VOYENNES to AUBOIR.	A.C.J.
AUBOIR.	23/4/17		Office. Visits 61st Mob Vet Sec. + Section of 61st D.A.C.	A.C.J.
"	24/4/17		Office Visits 2/3 Field Ambulance & 164 M.G. Co.	A.C.J.
"	25/4/17		Office. Visits 61st Mob Vet Sec.	A.C.J.
"	26/4/17		Office. Visits 2/3 Field Ambulance + 164 M.G.C.	A.C.J.
"	27/4/17		Office. Annuals D.H.R. Annuals also H.Q.C.R.A.	A.C.J.
"	28/4/17		Office. D.H.Q. + visits 61st Mob Vet Sec.	A.C.J.
"	29/4/17		Office Visits 61st Mob Vet Sec.	A.C.J.
"	30/4/17		Office. Annuals DH & Annuals + 61st Div Train A.S.C.	A.C.J.

J.E.C. Jones
Major
A.D.V.S. 61st Division

Confidential

Army Form C. 2118.

61st Division
May 1st 1914.

ADVS 8 bt /13

WAR DIARY
or
INTELLIGENCE SUMMARY.
(Erase heading not required.)

Instructions regarding War Diaries and Intelligence Summaries are contained in F.S. Regs., Part II. and the Staff Manual respectively. Title pages will be prepared in manuscript.

Place	Date	Hour	Summary of Events and Information	Remarks and references to Appendices
AUROIR	1/5/14	Office	Sa Arrivals at D.H.Q. & Signals	A.C.T
"	2/5/14	Office	Visited Mot Ver Section Personnel all arrivals there	A.C.T
"	3/5/14	Office	Attended Conference D.D.V.S. at A.H.Q.	A.C.T
"	4/5/14	Office	Conference of V. Os. Division	A.C.T
"	5/5/14	Office	Visited Mot Ver Sec. & 3rd Field Ambulance	A.C.T
"	6/5/14	Office	Sa Arrivals at D.H.Q. Visited Mot Ver Sec.	A.C.T
"	7/5/14	Office	Sa Arrivals of Signal Co.	A.C.T
"	8/5/14	Office	Sa Arrivals at D.H.Q.	A.C.T
"	9/5/14	Office	Inspected Animals of 7,2 & 4th Coy. 61st Div Train A.S.C.	A.C.T
"	10/5/14	Office	Attended G.O.C. Inspection of 1st Line Transport - Visited No.1 Co. Div Train A.S.C.	A.C.T
"	11/5/14	Office	Visited Mot Ver Sec.	A.C.T
"	12/5/14	Office	Inspected M.M.P. Horses, 306 Bde R.F.A. & 3rd Field Ambulance	A.C.T
"	13/5/14	Office	Visited Mot Ver Sec. & R.A. Hd Quarters	A.C.T
"	14/5/14	Office		A.C.T
"	15/5/14	Marched out of AUROIR		A.C.T
VIGNACOURT	16/5/14	Office opened at VIGNACOURT.		A.C.T

Confidential

61st Division
May 14th 1917

WAR DIARY
or
INTELLIGENCE SUMMARY.

Army Form C. 2118.

(Erase heading not required.)

Instructions regarding War Diaries and Intelligence Summaries are contained in F. S. Regs., Part II. and the Staff Manual respectively. Title pages will be prepared in manuscript.

Place	Date	Hour	Summary of Events and Information	Remarks and references to Appendices
VIGNACOURT	14/5/17	Office	Left for 10 days leave to England. Capt. A.W. REID. A.V.C. to act as A.D.V.S. while I am away.	A.G.T.
"	17/5/17			A.G.T.
"	18/5/17	Office	Inspected horses of H.Q. 3 Cy. divl. Train.	Aust R.
"	19/5/17	Office	Inspected lines of post M.2.	Aust R.
"	20/5/17	Office	Inspected lines 1/5 D.C.L.I.	Aust R.
DOULLENS	21/5/17	Office	Went to DOULLENS.	Aust R.
"	22/5/17	Office	Inspected 183 Infantry Bde & 2/2 Field Ambulance	Aust R.
LE CAUROY	23/5/17	Office	Went to LE CAUROY.	Aust R.
WARLUS	24/5/17	Office	Went to Warlus. Inspected 182 Infy 1 Bde Staff.	Aust R.
"	25/5/17	Office	Inspected D.H.Q. 183 & 184 Infy Bd grps.	Aust R.
"	26/5/17	Office	Visited M.V.S. 306 & 307 Ron. R.F.A. & OUTREBOIS.	Aust R.
"	27/5/17	Office	Visited 2/3 Field Amb, 476 Cy R.E. 8.1 Cy A.S.C. & D.A.C	Aust R.
"	28/5/17	Office	Visited 184 Infy Bde. & 61 Coy A.S.C.	Aust R.
"	29/5/17	Office	Inspected lines 2/4 Glohrs. 183/134 & 182 130 grps.	Aust R.
"	30/5/17	Office	Returned from leave took over from Capt. Reid A.V.C.	A.G.T.
"	31/5/17	Office	Inspected D.H.Q. Animals	A.G.T.

J.K.C. Jones
Major A.V.C.
A.D.V.S. 61st Division

Confidential

Army Form C. 2118.

WAR DIARY
or
INTELLIGENCE SUMMARY.
(Erase heading not required.)

A.D.V.S.,
61st (S.M.) DIVISION.
No. ....
Date 1/6/17.

Instructions regarding War Diaries and Intelligence Summaries are contained in F. S. Regs., Part II. and the Staff Manual respectively. Title pages will be prepared in manuscript.

Place	Date	Hour	Summary of Events and Information	Remarks and references to Appendices
WARLUS	1/6/17		Office.	A.C.J.
"	2/6/17		Office. Closed at WARLUS, reopened at ARRAS.	A.C.J.
ARRAS	3/6/17		Office. Advanced Conference of D.D.V.S. 3rd Army	A.C.J.
"	4/6/17		Visit to Divisional D.H.Q. & 17th & 19th Bde.	
"	5/6/17		" Visited 182 Inf. Bde.	
"	6/6/17		Office. Re Censure D.H.Q.	
"	7/6/17		" - Visited 183 Inf. Bde. Transport Nuisance	
"	8/6/17		Visit 183 Inf. Bde. No 3 Co A.S.C. & 498 - 499 Field Co. R.E	
"	9/6/17		Office. Re Nuisance D.H.Q. 445 & Signals &c.	
"	10/6/17		" Inspection 1st 2nd 3rd Indian Ambulances etc A.D.M.S.	
"	11/6/17		Office. Nuisance out of ARRAS. with D.H.Q. & WARLUS	
WARLUS	12/6/17		Office. Return to WARLUS. Rifles (at Mon 2.c. etc.)	
"			" - Visits 3rd E. Bde. R.F.A.	
"			" - Py H. & nuisance.	
"	23/6/17		Office. Visits ARRAS to interview A.D.V.S. 56th Division	9CJ
"	10/9/17		Office. Re Animals at D.H.Q.	A.C.J.

Confidential

Instructions regarding War Diaries and Intelligence Summaries are contained in F.S. Regs., Part II. and the Staff Manual respectively. Title pages will be prepared in manuscript.

WAR DIARY
or
INTELLIGENCE SUMMARY.
(Erase heading not required)

A.D.V.S.
61st Division Army Form C. 2118.
14/6/14.

Place	Date	Hour	Summary of Events and Information	Remarks and references to Appendices
WARLUS.	17/6/17		Office. & annuals 183 Inf Bde 179 Q.Co. Signals	JLCJ
"	18/6/17		Office. Go D.H.Q. annuals	JLCJ
"	19/6/17		Office. Visited 61st D.A.C. & 184 Inf Bde.	JLCJ
"	20/6/17		Office. Go D.H.Q. annuals 179 Q Co. Signals	JLCJ
"	21/6/17		Office. D.H.Q.	JLCJ
"	22/6/17		Office Go annuals 306 Bde R.F.A.	JLCJ
"	23/6/17		Marched from WARLUS. to WILLEMAN.	JLCJ
WILLEMAN	24/6/17		Office. Visited 61st Mot Vet Sec.	JLCJ
"	25/6/17		Office Visited 164 Inf Bde.	JLCJ
"	26/6/17		Office Visited Mot Vet Sec.	JLCJ
"	27/6/17		Office. Visited 184 Inf Bde.	JLCJ
"	28/6/17		Office Visited 2/1 Bucks - 2/5 Gloucesters - 2/4 Oxfords & Bucks - 2/4 Co Train A.S.C.	JLCJ
"	29/6/17		Office Visited 2/5 Gloucesters 3 Field Ambulance & 183 Machine Gun Co.	JLCJ
"	30/6/17		Office - Visited 2/4 Oxfords & Bucks	JLCJ

J. L. Jones
Major A.V.C.
A.D.V.S. 61st Division.

WAR DIARY
or
INTELLIGENCE SUMMARY.

Army Form C. 2118.

Place	Date	Hour	Summary of Events and Information	Remarks and references to Appendices
WILLEMAN	1/4/17	Office	Visited 2/4 Ot. & Bucks L.I. Mot. Vet. Sec.	A.C.O
"	2/4/17	Office	Visited Train A.S.C.	A.C.O
"	3/4/17	Office	Visited HQ Sig Co. + Divisional Art.	A.C.O
"	4/4/17	Office	Visited 164 Dy Bde.	A.C.O
"	5/4/17	Office	Visited Nos 445, 448, + 449 Cos. R.E.	A.C.O
"	6/4/17	Office	Visited Mot Vet-Sec. + H.Q. Sig Co.	A.C.O
"	7/4/17	Office	Visited 2/8 Worcesters	A.C.O
"	8/4/17	Office	62 D.H.Q. arrivals	A.C.O
"	9/4/17	Office	A.D.H.Q. arrivals	A.C.O
"	10/4/17	Office	Visited Mot.Vet.Sec. 3 Co. A.S.C. + 184 Dy Bde.	A.C.O
"	11/4/17	Office	Visited 2/3 Field Ambulance	A.C.O
"	12/4/17	Office	Visited Mot Vet Sec.	A.C.O
"	13/4/17	Office	Visited Mot Vet Co. 1/54 Machine Gun Co.	A.C.O
"	14/4/17	Office	" Mot Vet Sec. + 2/4 Gloucester Rgt.	A.C.O
"	15/4/17	Office	" Mot Vet-Sec.	A.C.O
"	16/4/17	Office	" Mot Vet-Sec.	A.C.O

WAR DIARY or INTELLIGENCE SUMMARY

Army Form C. 2118.

Place	Date	Hour	Summary of Events and Information	Remarks and references to Appendices
WILLEMAN	17/7/17		Office - Visited Mot. Vet. Sec.	A.C.A.
"	18/4/17		Office - to H.Q. Hours.	A.C.A.
"	19/4/17		Office - Visited Mot Vet Sec.	A.C.A.
"	20/4/17		Office. Visit Vet Sec.	A.C.A.
"	21/4/17		Office. Visit Vet Sec. D.H.Q. anivals	A.C.A.
"	22/4/17		Office. Visit Vet Sec. + N° 2 Co Train A.S.C.	A.C.A.
"	23/4/17		Office - Visited 3rd Field Ambulance + 2/6 Gloster Regt.	A.C.A.
"	24/4/17		Office - Visited Mot Vet Sec.	A.C.A.
"	25/4/17		Moved out from WILLEMAN with D.H.Q. owned ZEGGERS CAPEL.	A.C.A.
"	26/4/17		Office. Visited 4/8 Field A.B.S + 2/6 Worcesters	A.C.A.
ZEGGERS CAPPEL	27/4/17		Office - Attended Conference VIII Corps.	A.C.A.
"	28/4/17		Office.	A.C.A.
"	29/4/17		Office. Visited 184 Inf. Bde.	A.C.A.
"	30/4/17		Office. Visited 4/6 Fields & R.E. + 2/8 Worcester Regt.	A.C.A.
"	31/4/17		Office. Visited 4/6 Worcester Regt. Divisional Transport.	A.C.A.

J.E. Orr
Major A.V.C.
A.D.V.S. 61st Division.

Confidential

A.D.V.S.
61st (S.M.) DIVISION.
No. ....
Date. 1/9/17

WAR DIARY
or
INTELLIGENCE SUMMARY.
(Erase heading not required.)

Army Form C. 2118.

Instructions regarding War Diaries and Intelligence Summaries are contained in F. S. Regs., Part II. and the Staff Manual respectively. Title pages will be prepared in manuscript.

Place	Date	Hour	Summary of Events and Information	Remarks and references to Appendices
ZEGGERS.CAPPEL.	1/8/17		Office. Visited D.H.Q. annexes. H.Q. Signals & H.Q. 61st Div. Train. A.S.C.	K.C.J.
"	2/8/17		Office. Visited 2/8 Worcesters Regt. 478 C.F.E. 1/83 Machine Gun Co.	K.C.J.
"	3/8/17		Office. Visited D.H.Q. annexes. H.Q Signal Co. & C.R.E.	K.C.J.
"	4/8/17		Office. Attended Conference VIII CORPS. Visited 61st Mot. Vet. Sec. 478 R.E. Co.	K.C.J.
"	5/8/17		Office. Visited 478 Field Co. R.E.	K.C.J.
"	6/8/17		Office. Attended Training Operation 182 Inf. Bde. Attended Gas Parade D.H.Q.	K.C.J.
"	7/8/17		Office. Visited No. 4 Co. Train A.S.C. & 2/8 Worcester Regt. also D.H.Q. annexes	K.C.J.
"	8/8/17		Office. Visited Mot. Vet. Sec. Inspected Remounts at No.4 Co. Train A.S.C.	K.C.J.
"	9/8/17		Office. Inspected Animals of 1/83 Machine Gun Co. 478 & 476 Field Co. R.E.	K.C.J.
"	10/8/17		Office. Visited D.H.Q. annexes & H.Q Signals Co.	K.C.J.
"	11/8/17		Office. Attended Conference at 8th CORPS.	K.C.J.
"	12/8/17		Office. Visited H.Q. 61st Divisional Train A.S.C.	K.C.J.
"	13/8/17		Office. Visited 2/8 Worcester Regt. Mot. Vet. Sec. 61st Division.	K.C.J.
"	14/8/17		Office. Visited 478 F.A. Field Co. R.E. 1/83 Machine Gun Co.	K.C.J.
"	15/8/17		Marched from ZEGGERS.CAPPEL. to POPERINGHE. Reported to A.D.V.S. 19th CORPS.	K.C.J.
POPERINGHE.	16/8/17		Office. Visited 19th CORPS.	K.C.J.

Confidential

Army Form C. 2118.

A.D.V.S.
61st (S.M.) DIVISION.
No. ....
Date 14-8-17.

WAR DIARY
or
INTELLIGENCE SUMMARY.
(Erase heading not required.)

Instructions regarding War Diaries and Intelligence Summaries are contained in F. S. Regs., Part II. and the Staff Manual respectively. Title pages will be prepared in manuscript.

Place	Date	Hour	Summary of Events and Information	Remarks and references to Appendices
POPERINGHE.	14/8/17		Visited A.D.V.S. 19th CORPS. & Site for Advance Veterinary Aid Post at H.11.b.9.9. Sheet 28. O.C.C.S.	H.C.J.
"	15/8/17		Moved from POPERINGHE to MERSEY CAMP. H.1. Sheet 28.	H.C.J.
MERSEY CAMP.	19/8/17		Office. Visited 476 & 478. F.A. R.E. also Mob. Vet. Sec. at G.11.a.4.b. Sheet 28.	H.C.J.
"	20/8/17		Office. Visited 306 & 307 Bde. R.F.A. Inspected Animals for Evacuation	H.C.J.
"	21/8/17		Visited 61st D.A.C. Inspected animals for Evacuation	H.C.J.
"	22/8/17		Office. Visited 61st Mob. Vet. Sec. & D.H.Q. Animals	H.C.J.
"	23/8/17		Office. Visited 61st Mob. Vet. Sec. Inspected Animals	H.C.J.
"	24/8/17		Office. Visited 61st Mob. Vet. Sec. 476 & 478 R.E. & M.M.P.	H.C.J.
"	25/8/17		Office. Visited 61st Mob. Vet. Sec. 19th Corps Troops Control. & M.M.P. Inspected Animals	H.C.J.
"	26/8/17		Visited 61st Mob. Vet. Sec. & a Itre Q animals 61st Div.	H.C.J.
"	27/8/17		Office. Visited 61st Mob. Vet. Sec. Returned Office A.D.V.S. XIX CORPS.	H.C.J.
"	28/8/17		Office. Sec D.H.Q. animals Signal Co.	H.C.J.
"	29/8/17		Office. & Inspecting Transport of the Division	H.C.J.
"	30/8/17		Office. Visited 61st Mob. Vet. Sec.	H.C.J.
"	31/8/17		Office. Conference with V.Os. 61st Division	H.C.J.

J.L.C. Jones
Major A.V.C.
D.A.D.V.S. 61st Division.

Confidential

Army Form C. 2118.

WAR DIARY
or
INTELLIGENCE SUMMARY.

(Erase heading not required.)

D.A.D.V.S.,
61st
DIVISION.
Date 29/10/19

Place	Date	Hour	Summary of Events and Information	Remarks and references to Appendices
ARRAS.	30/10/19	Office		A.C.I.
"	31/10/19	Office	Visited 61st D.A.C. howitzer & horses arrived.	O.C.C.
			3rd Army. The Divisional Artillery was inspected by D.D.V.S. during the month, the expressed himself as being very satisfied with their condition all round. Infantry Transport was inspected by A.D.V.S. 14th Corps who was also very satisfied.	
			J.C.C.Mac. Major AVC. D.A.D.V.S. 61st Division.	

Confidential

Army Form C. 2118.

D.A.D.V.S.
61st
DIVISION.
No. ....
Date 1/11/17

WAR DIARY
or
INTELLIGENCE SUMMARY.
(Erase heading not required.)

Instructions regarding War Diaries and Intelligence Summaries are contained in F.S. Regs., Part II. and the Staff Manual respectively. Title pages will be prepared in manuscript.

Place	Date	Hour	Summary of Events and Information	Remarks and references to Appendices
ARRAS.	1/11/17		Office. Conference with V.Os. of the Division – Visits 61st Mob. Vet. Sec.	A.C.I.
"	2/11/17		Office. Visits 184 Bde. Inspected Animals Standings, also 479 Feles & R.E.	A.C.I.
"	3/11/17		Office.	A.C.I.
"	4/11/17		Office. Mobile Vet – Sec. & 2/3 Field Ambulance. Inspected Animals	A.C.I.
"	5/11/17		Office.	A.C.I.
"	6/11/17		Office. Visits 2/1 & 2/2 Field Ambulances.	A.C.I.
"	7/11/17		Office. Visits 61st Mob. Vet. Sec.	A.C.I.
"	8/11/17		Office. Conference with V.Os. 61st Division	A.C.I.
"	9/11/17		Office. Visits Mob. Vet. Sec. – C.R.A. & 2/4 Wonceslin. Inspected Animals	A.C.I.
"	10/11/17		Office. Visits Mob. Vet. Sec. Sic Animals of 61st D.A.C.	A.C.I.
"	11/11/17		Office. Visits Mob. Vet. Sec.	A.C.I.
"	12/11/17		Office. Visits 1st Line Transport into D.A.Q.M.G. Inspected Animals Standings	A.C.I.
"	13/11/17		Office. Visits Inspected Animals 306 Bde R.F.A.	A.C.I.
"	14/11/17		Office. Visits Inspected Animals 307 Bde R.F.A. Visits Mob. Vet. Sec.	A.C.I.
"	15/11/17		Office. Conference V.Os. of the Division	A.C.I.
"	16/11/17		Office. Inspected Animals of Divisional Train A.S.C. Visits Mob. Vet. Sec.	A.C.I.

Confidential

Army Form C. 2118.

WAR DIARY
or
INTELLIGENCE SUMMARY.
(Erase heading not required.)

Instructions regarding War Diaries and Intelligence Summaries are contained in F. S. Regs., Part II. and the Staff Manual respectively. Title pages will be prepared in manuscript.

D.A.D.V.S., 61st DIVISION.
No. ....
Date 17-11-17.

Vol 19

Place	Date	Hour	Summary of Events and Information	Remarks and references to Appendices
ARRAS.	17/11/17		Office. Attended Conference A.D.V.S. 19th Corps. Visited 61st Mob. Vet. Sec.	H.C.J.
"	18/11/17		Office. Visited 2/8 Field Ambulance — also Mob. Vet. Sec. Inspected Horses.	J.E.C.J.
"	19/11/17		Office. Visited 2/5. D.C.L.I. Inspected Transport Animals, also 2/4 Worcesters.	J.E.C.J.
"	20/11/17		Office. To annual T.M.M.P.	H.C.J.
"	21/11/17		Office. Visited Mob. Vet. Sec. Mob. Quarter Signals B. Yell Hor Quarter Stores.	H.C.J.
"	22/11/17		Office. Conference of Vety officers of the Division.	H.C.J.
"	23/11/17		Office. Visited Mob. Vet. Sec.	H.C.J.
"	24/11/17		Office. Attended Conference at Office A.D.V.S. 19th Corps.	J.C.J.
"	25/11/17		Office. Visited 304 Bde R.F.A. Head Quarters R.A. Beaumes Animals	H.C.J.
"	26/11/17		Office. Attended Inspection by A.D.V.S. 19th Corps. 304 Bde R.F.A. Mob. D.A.C.	H.C.d.
"	27/11/17		Office. Visited 61st Mob. Vet. Sec.	H.C.d.
"	28/11/17		Office. Visited 61st Mob. Vet. Sec. Inspected Personnel.	H.C.d.
"	29/11/17		Office. Visited 61st Mob. Vet. Sec.	H.C.d.
"	30/11/17		Marched from ARRAS. to YTRES.	H.C.d.

H.C.Ihee
Major A.V.C.
D.A.D.V.S. 61st Division

Confidential
Army Form C. 2118.

Instructions regarding War Diaries and Intelligence Summaries are contained in F. S. Regs., Part II. and the Staff Manual respectively. Title pages will be prepared in manuscript.

WAR DIARY
or
INTELLIGENCE SUMMARY.
(Erase heading not required.)

D.A.D.V.S.
51st DIVISION
Date 1/12/14

JM 20

Place	Date	Hour	Summary of Events and Information	Remarks and references to Appendices
YTRES.	1/12/14		Arrived here on the night of the 30th ult. moved to ETRICOURT. Early morning 1-12-14	A.C.d.
ETRICOURT.	2/12/14		Visited D.A.D.V.S. 30th Division re taking over.	A.C.d.
"	3/12/14		Visited 1st line transport.	A.C.d.
"	4/12/14		Office. Visited 61st Divisional Train A.S.C. & 61st Mot Hor Sec.	A.C.d.
"	5/12/14		Office. Attended Office A.D.V.S. Third Corps.	A.C.d.
"	6/12/14		Office. Went round Area.	A.C.d.
"	7/12/14		Office. Visited 236 Bde R.F.A. re Stomatitis, by order A.D.V.S. Third Corps. returned.	A.C.d.
"	8/12/14		Office. Inspection Removals.	A.C.d.
"	9/12/14		Office. Interviewed D.A.D.V.S. 49th Division by order A.D.V.S. Third Corps. held Coy Inspection.	A.C.d.
"	10/12/14		Office. Visited D.H.Q. Horses. No 9 Signal Co. 1st Dn Mot Hor Sec & 306 Bde R.F.A.	A.C.d.
"	11/12/14		Office. Visited proposed standing for D.A.C. 61st Div. with A.A.G.	A.C.d.
"	12/12/14		Office. Inspection 306 Bde R.F.A. animals standing separate fairly well.	A.C.d.
"	13/12/14		Office. Conference with Vety Officers of the Division. Visited 61st Mot Hor Sec.	A.C.d.
"	14/12/14		Office. Visited 61st Mot Hor Sec re Evacuations	A.C.d.
"	15/12/14		Office. Reported to 3rd Corps.	A.C.d.
"	16/12/14		Office. Visited 307 Bde R.F.A.	A.C.V.

Confidential

Army Form C. 2118.

WAR DIARY
or
INTELLIGENCE SUMMARY.
(Erase heading not required.)

D.A.D.V.S.
61st
DIVISION.

No. ....
Date 74/12/17.

Instructions regarding War Diaries and Intelligence Summaries are contained in F. S. Regs., Part II. and the Staff Manual respectively. Title pages will be prepared in manuscript.

Place	Date	Hour	Summary of Events and Information	Remarks and references to Appendices
ETRICOURT.	17/12/17		Office.	A.C.O
"	18/12/17		Office.	A.C.O
"	19/12/17		Office. Inspected 2nd Troop's Cavalry Squadron & 19th Reserve Park's	A.C.O
"	20/12/17		Office. Inspected Northumberland Hussars. Conference V.O. 6th Division.	A.C.O
"	21/12/17.		Office. Attended Conference	A.C.O
"	22/12/17		Office. Inspected 61st Divisional Train Horses.	A.C.O
"	23/12/17.		Marched from ETRICOURT to MERICOURT. SUR. SOMME.	A.C.O
MERICOURT.	24/12/17		Office.	A.C.O
"	25/12/17		Office. Visited 161st Inst. Vet. Billet at ETINEHEM.	A.C.O
"	26/12/17		Office. Visited 61st Labour Group. & 46 P. of War Co. Camp. Inspected Animals	A.C.O
"	27/12/17		Office. Visited 61st Inst. Vet.	H.C.O
"	28/12/17		Office. Inspected D.H.Q. Animals	A.C.O
"	29/12/17		Office.	A.C.O
"	30/12/17		Office.	A.C.O
"	31/12/17		Marched from MERICOURT. to HARBONNIERS.	A.C.O

H.C.Price
Major A.V.C.
D.A.D.V.S. 61st Division

Confidential

Army Form C. 2118.

WAR DIARY
or
INTELLIGENCE SUMMARY.
(Erase heading not required.)

A.D.V.S.
61st
Division.

No. .... Date 1/1/18

Place	Date	Hour	Summary of Events and Information	Remarks and references to Appendices
HARBONNIÈRES	1/1/18	Office.	Visited animals of Divisional Headquarters, also Mob. Vety. Sec.	OKCd
"	2/1/18	Office.		OKCd
"	3/1/18	Office.	Conference with V.Os. of Division	OKCd
"	4/1/18	Office.	Visited 61st Mob. Vet. Sec.	OKCd
"	5/1/18	Office.	Visited Mob. Vet. Sec.	OKCd
"	6/1/18	Office.	Visited Mob. Vet. Sec. & D.V.Q. animals	OKCd
"	7/1/18	Arena	with D.V.Q. to NESLE.	OKCd
NESLE.	8/1/18	Office.	Inspected French Stables at Mangy.	OKCd
"	9/1/18	Office.	Visited D.V.Q. animals – Inspected DAC animals 61st Div.	OKCd
"	10/1/18	Office.	Visited D.V.Q. animals – Inspected 306 Bde R.F.A. on the March	OKCd
"	11/1/18	Office.	Visited 61st Mob. Vet. Sec.	OKCd
"	12/1/18	Moved	from NESLE to AUBOIR.	OKCd
AUBOIR.	13/1/18	Office.	Inspected Standing Stables AFF at FORESTE.	OKCd
"	14/1/18	Office.	Inspected D.V.Q. animals	OKCd
"	15/1/18	Office.	Inspected animals 2nd Traffic Con Squadron –	OKCd
"	16/1/18	Office.	Visited Mob. Vet. Sec. + H.Q. Signal Co.	OKCd

2353 Wt. W2544/1454 700,000 5/15 D.D. & L. A.D.S.S./Forms/C. 2118.

Army Form C. 2118.

WAR DIARY
or
INTELLIGENCE SUMMARY.
(Erase heading not required.)

D.A.D.V.S.
61st DIVISION
19/1/18.

Place	Date	Hour	Summary of Events and Information	Remarks and references to Appendices
AUROIR.	17/1/18		Office. Inspected D.T.Q animals. Conference D.V.O.s.	ACS
"	18/1/18		Office. Inspected D.T.Q. animals	ACD
"	19/1/18		Office. Visited Mot. Vet Sec & 183 Iny Bde.	ACD
"	20/1/18		Office. Visited 264 Machine Gun Co.	ACD
"	21/1/18		Office. Visited 315 Heavy Arty Bde.	ACD
"	22/1/18		Office. Inspected 111th Heavy Batt.	ACD
"	23/1/18		Office. Visited 315 Arty Bde.	ACD
"	24/1/18		Office. Conference V.Os. 61st Division	JCD
"	25/1/18		Office. Inspected animals 61st Div Train A.S.C.	JCD
"	26/1/18		Office. Sauvoes animals at D.T.Q.	JCD
"	27/1/18		Office. Visited 61st D.A.C. Inspected animals	ACS
"	28/1/18		Office - Inspected D.T.Q. Stores - Visited 61st Mot Vet Sec. & animals for evacuation.	JCCS
"	29/1/18		Office. Inspected animals 2/3 Field Ambulance & 315 13A.C. A.F.A.	JCCJ
"	30/1/18		Office. Inspected animals 304 Bde R.F.A. 449 J.C. R.J. & 181 M Gun Co	JCD
"	31/1/18		Office. Inspected animals 61st Train A.S.C. with AA & Q.M.G.	ACD

J.L.C. Snee
Major A.V.C.
D.A.D.V.S. 61st Division.

Confidential

Army Form C. 2118.

WAR DIARY
or
INTELLIGENCE SUMMARY.

(Erase heading not required.)

D.A.D.V.S.,
61st
DIVISION.
Date ...1/7/18...

Place	Date	Hour	Summary of Events and Information	Remarks and references to Appendices
AVOIR	1/2/18	Office	Visited 61st D.A.C.	A.C.I.
"	2/2/18	Office	Sc annual at D.T.V.R.	A.C.I.
"	3/2/18	Office	Sc annual N.Q. Sig re C. Visited 61st Mob Vet Sec	A.C.I.
"	4/2/18	Office	Visited 61st Mob Vet Sec. Sc annual for Evacuation	A.C.I.
"	5/2/18	Office	Inspected 1st Res Transport 2/4th Gloucester. 2/6th Rifle Worcester.	A.C.I.
			Inspected 1st Div Transport 5th Gordons by joining Division	A.C.I.
"	6/2/18	Office	& D.T.V.R. annual - Visited GERMAINE le Transport Lines &c.	J.C.I.
"	7/2/18	Office	Conference with V.Os. of the Division - Visited Mob Vet Sec.	J.C.I.
"	8/2/18	Office	Visited 264 Machine Gun Co & 93 Field Ambulance. Inspected animals	J.C.I.
"	9/2/18	Office	Visited 2/1 Field Ambulance.	J.C.I.
"	10/2/18	Office	Visited H field annual. D.T.V.R. annual	A.C.I.
"	11/2/18	Office	Visited 306 Pack R.T.Q. & 61st Mob Vet Sec	J.C.I.
"	12/2/18	Office	Sc annual at D.T.V.R. Attended Station of Evacuation	J.C.I.
"	13/2/18	Office	Interview with A.D.V.S. 16th Corps	A.C.I.
"	14/2/18	Office	Conference with V.Os. of Division. Visited 61st Mob Vet Sec	A.C.I.
"	15/2/18	Office	Visited 200th Field & R.E. inspected animals	J.C.I.

Confidential

Army Form C. 2118.

WAR DIARY
or
INTELLIGENCE SUMMARY.
(Erase heading not required.)

Instructions regarding War Diaries and Intelligence Summaries are contained in F.S. Regs., Part II. and the Staff Manual respectively. Title pages will be prepared in manuscript.

D.A.D.V.S.
61st DIVISION.
No. 16/2/18

Place	Date	Hour	Summary of Events and Information	Remarks and references to Appendices
AUBIGNY.	16/2/18		Office. Scanned Animals at D.H.Q.	JEJ
"	17/2/18		Office. Scanned Arrival at A.T.Q.	JEJ
"	18/2/18		Office. Visited 306 Bde R.F.A.	JEJ
"	19/2/18		Office. Visited 61st D.A.C. & 315 B.A.C.	JEJ
	20/2/18		Office.	JEJ
	21/2/18		Office. Conference D.Os. of Division. Scanned Animals at 61st Mot. P. Sec.	JEJ
	22/2/18		Office. Visited 315 Bde A.F.A.	JEJ
	23/2/18		Office. Attended Conference A.D.V.S. XVIII Corps.	JEJ
	24/2/18		Office. Visited 61st Mot. V. Sec. Inspected some 1st Line Transport Horses.	JCJ
	25/2/18		Office. Visited 61st M.V. Sec. & C Bato. 307 Bde R.F.A. with A.D.V.S. XVIII Corps	JCJ
	26/2/18		Office. Scanned Remounts R.F.A. Visited 61st D.A.C.	JCJ
	27/2/18		Office. Visited 61st Mot. V. Sec.	JCJ
	28/2/18		Office. Conference I.Os. of Division. Visited 61st Mot. V. Sec. Scanned Animals for Evacuation.	JCJ

J.E.Cone.
Major A.V.C.
D.A.D.V.S. 61st Division.

Confidential
Army Form C. 2118.

WAR DIARY
or
INTELLIGENCE SUMMARY.

(Erase heading not required.)

61st DIVISION. March 1st 1918.

VA 23

Place	Date	Hour	Summary of Events and Information	Remarks and references to Appendices
AUROIR.	1/3/18		Office. Visited Machine Gun Bn.	JCCJ
	2/3/18		Office. 61 DTR Annuals.	JCCJ
	3/3/18		Office. Visited 61st Mot Vet Sec	JCCJ
	4/3/18		Office. Visited 61st Mot Vet Sec. Animals post mortems	JCCJ
	5/3/18		Office. Visited BEAUVOIR. VILLEVEQUE re. re Advanced Aid Post & Tunnies	JCCJ
	—		— Moves for Evacuation of wounded to Mot Vet Sec.	JCCJ
	6/3/18		Office 6c DTR.A. annuals	JCCJ
	7/3/18		Office Conference with Dos Division. Visited 61st Mot Vet Sec	JCCJ
	8/3/18		Office Inspected 306 Bde R.F.A. Annuals.	JCCJ
	9/3/18		Office	JCCJ
	10/3/18		Office. Visited 61st Mot Vet Sec.	JCCJ
	11/3/18		Office. Inspected Animals 61st D.A.C.	JCCJ
	12/3/18		Office. Inspect 1st Line Transport 183 dy Bde. also C/304 Bde R.F.A.	JCCJ
	13/3/18		Office. Visited 61st Mot Vet Sec. Attended Conference ADMS XVIII Corps	JCCJ
	14/3/18		Office. Proceeded on 14 days leave to England. "Blackdown AKC	JCCJ
			Offr 61st Mot Vet Sec to carry on my duties while I am on leave.	JCCJ

WAR DIARY
or
INTELLIGENCE SUMMARY.
(Erase heading not required.)

Army Form C. 2118.

Instructions regarding War Diaries and Intelligence Summaries are contained in F. S. Regs., Part II. and the Staff Manual respectively. Title pages will be prepared in manuscript.

Place	Date	Hour	Summary of Events and Information	Remarks and references to Appendices
AUBOIR	15/3/18		Assisted duties of Office, visited Signals & hors of D.H.Q. Staff.	G.W.B.
"	16/3/18		Attended duties of Office. visited 6144 M.G. Battalion	G.W.B.
"	17/3/18		Attended duties of Office, visited Signals & D.H.Q.	G.W.B.
"	18.3.18		Attended duties of Office. visited 1st Line Transport 162 Inf Brigade	G.W.B.
"	19.3.18		Attended duties of Office, visited Signals, D.H.Q. 306, 307 Brigades. R.F.A.	G.W.B.
"	20.3.18		Attended duties of Office, visited work.	G.W.B.
"	21.3.18		Attended to duties of Office. Complete tilt instruction re manning Battle Zone on opening of Enemy offensive, instructed Aid Post at VILLEVEQUE, withdrew same at night for billeting reasons.	G.W.B.
"	22.3.18		D.H.Q moved to RETHONVILLERS.	G.W.B.
RETHONVILLERS	23.3.18		Attended duties of Office, visited D.H.Q.	G.W.B.
PARVILLERS	24.3.18		D.H.Q moved to PARVILLERS. Attended duties of Office.	G.W.B.
BEAUCOURT	25.3.18		D.H.Q moved to BEAUCOURT en Santerre.	G.W.B.
" en Santerre	26.3.18		Attended duties of Office.	G.W.B.
"	27.3.18		Attended duties of Office, visited D.H.Q. Signals.	G.W.B.
VILLERS BRETON NEUX	28.3.18		D.H.Q. moved to VILLERS-BRETONNEUX.	G.W.B.
BOVES	29.3.18		D.H.Q. moved to BOVES.	G.W.B.

Army Form C. 2118.

WAR DIARY
or
INTELLIGENCE SUMMARY.
(Erase heading not required.)

Instructions regarding War Diaries and Intelligence Summaries are contained in F. S. Regs., Part II. and the Staff Manual respectively. Title pages will be prepared in manuscript.

Place	Date	Hour	Summary of Events and Information	Remarks and references to Appendices
BOVES	28.3.18		Attended to duties of Office	G.4.B
"	29.3.18		Attended to duties of Office, visited D.H.Q Signals.	G.4.B
"	30.3.18		Attended to duties of Office, inspected baths at COTTENCHY.	G.4.B
"	31.3.18		Attended to duties of Office	

J.H. Blossom
Capt. R.A.M.C.

Confidential

Army Form C. 2118.

D.A.D.V.S.
61st DIVISION

WAR DIARY
or
INTELLIGENCE SUMMARY.

(Erase heading not required.)

Instructions regarding War Diaries and Intelligence Summaries are contained in F. S. Regs., Part II. and the Staff Manual respectively. Title pages will be prepared in manuscript.

Place	Date	Hour	Summary of Events and Information	Remarks and references to Appendices
BOVES.	1/4/18		D.J.V.S. at BOVES.	A.C.J
"	2/4/18		Returned from leave. Took over duties.	A.C.J
PISSY.	3/4/18		Marched from BOVES. hrs. arrived about midnight	A.C.J
"	4/4/18		Office. Re D.J.V.S. annual.	A.C.J
"	5/4/18		Office. St D.J.V.S. annual.	A.C.J
"	6/4/18		Office. St D.J.V.S. annual.	A.C.J
"	7/4/18		Office. Visited 182 Inf Bde	A.C.J
"	8/4/18		Office. Mob Vet Sec. moved to ARGUEL.	A.C.J
"	9/4/18		Office	A.C.J
"	10/4/18		Moved from PISSY. to AIRE.	A.C.J
AIRE.	11/4/18		Arrived with D.J.V.S. at AIRE.	A.C.J
"	12/4/18		Office. Visited 11th Corps. Veterinary Evacuation Station under instruction A.D.V.S. Corps	A.C.J
"	13/4/18		Office. ditto	A.C.J
"	14/4/18		Office. ditto ditto	A.C.J
"	15/4/18		Office. " "	A.C.J
"	19/4/18		Office.	S.C.J

Confidential

Army Form C. 2118.

WAR DIARY
or
INTELLIGENCE SUMMARY.
(Erase heading not required.)

Instructions regarding War Diaries and Intelligence Summaries are contained in F.S. Regs., Part II. and the Staff Manual respectively. Title pages will be prepared in manuscript.

D.A.D.V.S., 61st DIVISION.
Date 17/4/16

Place	Date	Hour	Summary of Events and Information	Remarks and references to Appendices
AIRE.	17/4/16	Office	Attended Corps Vnee Station. Inspected Animals for Inoculation	JCCJ
"	18/4/16	Office	"	JCCJ
"	19/4/16	Office	"	JCCJ
"	20/4/16	Office	"	JCCJ
"	21/4/16	Office	"	JCCJ
"	22/4/16	Office	"	JCCJ
"	23/4/16	Office	" Attended 11th Corps Conference	JCCJ
"	24/4/16	Office	"	JCCJ
"	25/4/16	Office	Att. Corps Vnee Station with D.D.V.S. 1st Army VADVS. 11th Corps, also Col. M.V.S.	JCCJ
"	26/4/16	Office	Attended with ADVC 11th Corps. Inspected 182 Sy Bde Hrs Train A.S.C.	JCCJ
"	27/4/16	Office	S.C. Drug Annuals	JCCJ
"	28/4/16	Office		JCCJ
"	29/4/16	Office	Inspected Animals of 306 & 309 Bdes R.F.A. also 61st D.A.C.	JCCJ
"	30/4/16	Office	Inspected Animals R.N.R.	JCCJ

J.C.C. Jones
Major A.V.C.
D.A.D.V.S. 61st Division.

Confidential

Army Form C. 2118.

WAR DIARY
or
INTELLIGENCE SUMMARY.

(Erase heading not required.)

D.A.D.V.S.
61st DIVISION.

Date 1/5/18.

Place	Date	Hour	Summary of Events and Information	Remarks and references to Appendices
AIRE.	1/5/18		Office. Visited XI Corps Evacuating Station. Rang A.D.V.S. Corps. Interview re animals.	JCCJ
"	2/5/18		Office. Inspected 163 & 184 Hy Bdes. Small Arms Section & Machine Gun Batt.	JCCJ
"	3/5/18		Office. Attended Inspection of A.D.V.S. 11th Corps. of 306 & 309 Bde R.F.A.	JCCJ
"	4/5/18		Office. Visited 61st Mob Vet Sec & 2/3 Field Ambulance	JCCJ
"	5/5/18		Office. Visited 306 Bde R.F.A.	JCCJ
"	6/5/18		Office. Attended Field Service Court Martial on A.V.C. private	JCCJ
"	7/5/18		Office. Visited 11th Corps Veterinary Evacuating Station	JCCJ
"	8/5/18		Office. Sic D.V.R. animals	JCCJ
"	9/5/18		Office. Visited 12th Australian Art Bde in company with A.D.V.S. 11th Corps	JCCJ
"	10/5/18		Office. Visited 61st Mob Vet Sec. Met D.D.R. 1st ARMY.	JCCJ
"	11/5/18		Office. Visited 61st Mob Vet Sec & 11th Corps V.E.S.	JCCJ
"	12/5/18		Office. Visited Forward Area with A.D.M.S. re dead animals unburied	JCCJ
"	13/5/18		Office. Examined D.T.R. animals	JCCJ
"	14/5/18		Office.	JCCJ
"	15/5/18		Office. Visited 61st Division Train. Inspected Surplus animals before departure.	JCCJ
"	16/5/18		Office. Examined D.T.R. animals	JCCJ

Confidential   Army Form C. 2118.

Instructions regarding War Diaries and Intelligence Summaries are contained in F.S. Regs., Part II. and the Staff Manual respectively. Title pages will be prepared in manuscript.

WAR DIARY
or
INTELLIGENCE SUMMARY.
(Erase heading not required.)

DIVS.
DIVISION
No. ....
Date .... 17/5/18 ....

Place	Date	Hour	Summary of Events and Information	Remarks and references to Appendices
AIRE.	17/5/18		Office.	JCCJ
"	18/5/18		Office. Moved from AIRE to LAMBRES.	JCCJ
LAMBRES.	19/5/18		Office. Visited 61st Div Train A.S.C.	JCCJ
"	20/5/18		Office. Visited 61st Mob Vet Sec. Examined R.V.A. animals	JCCJ
"	21/5/18		Office. Visited 61st Mob Vet Sec.	JCCJ
"	22/5/18		Office. Se N.V.A. animals	JCCJ
"	23/5/18		Office.	JCCJ
"	24/5/18		Office. Conference V.Os. Division Attacked troops. Visited advanced H.Q. Inspected Horses	JCCJ
"	25/5/18		Office. Visited 61st Mob Vet Sec. St D.V.T.R. animals	JCCJ
"	26/5/18		Office. Inspected 182 & 184 Dy Transport. Visited Office A.D.V.S. XI Corps	JCCJ
"	27/5/18		Office. Visited 61st Mob Vet Soc.	JCCJ
"	28/5/18		Office. Inspected 9 Northumberland Fus. 11th Supports & 1st E Lancs Transport on moving to Division	JCCJ
"	29/5/18		Office. Visited 61st Div Train A.S.C. Inspected Animals	JCCJ
"	30/5/18		Office. Visited Advanced H.Q. & 61st Mob Vet Sec 5c animals	JCCJ
"	30/5/18		Office. Visited 306 Bde R.F.A. & 262 Bde B.A.C.	JCCJ
"	31/5/18		Office. Visited 61st Mob Vet Sec. Inspected animals. C/262 Bde A.F.A.	JCCJ

J.C.C. Jones
Major. A.V.C.
D.A.D.V.S. 61st Div

WAR DIARY
or
INTELLIGENCE SUMMARY.

(Erase heading not required.)

D.A.D.V.S. Army Form C. 2118.
61st DIVISION.
Date: 1/9/18

Place	Date	Hour	Summary of Events and Information	Remarks and references to Appendices
LAMBRES.	1/9/18	Office.	At D.H.Q. Annuals.	J.R.C.J
"	2/9/18	Office.	At D.H.Q Annuals. Visited 61st Mob Vet Sec	J.R.C.J
"	3/9/18	Office.	Visited 61st D.A.C. Inspected annuals	J.R.C.J
"	4/9/18	Office.	Visited 61st Mob Vet Sec. Inspected annuals for Evacuation.	J.R.C.J
"	5/9/18	Office.	Visited 61st Mob Vet Sec. No Q Signal Co. & annuals.	J.R.C.J
"	6/9/18	Office.	Inspected annuals of 262 Bde A.F.A. with A.D.V.S. XI Corps	J.R.C.J
"	7/9/18	Office.	Visited 61st Mob Vet Sec. & annuals at D.H.Q.	J.R.C.J
"	8/9/18	Office.	At annuals at D.H.Q. Attended Conference A.D's + XI Corps.	J.R.C.J
"	9/9/18	Office.	Visited 61st M.V.S. Attended Conference A.D.V.S. XI Corps.	J.R.C.J
"	10/9/18	Office.	Inspected annuals of 282 Bde A.F.A. & 184 Bgl Bde Transport Lines.	J.R.C.J
"	11/9/18	Office.	Visited 61st Mob Vet Sec. Visited Transport Lines 2/4 Oxfords & 2/4 Berks.	J.R.C.J
"	12/9/18	Office.	Visited 61st M.V.S. Farriers annuals for Evacuation. Attend Pris horse Bat.	J.R.C.J
"	13/9/18	Office.	Inspected 61st M.V.S. with A.D.V.S. XI Corps. Visited Evacuation 282 Bde A.F.A.	J.R.C.J
"			— Inspected Evn Deaus hire, also the standing — Visited C/262 Inspected all annuals. Visited Bde M.T. Q.	J.R.C.J J.R.C.J
"	14/9/18	Office.	Visited 61st M.V.S. Inspected annuals for Evacuation. D.D.V.S. 1st Army Inspected 61st Mot Vet Sec.	J.R.C.J J.R.C.J

Confidential

Army Form C. 2113.

WAR DIARY
or
INTELLIGENCE SUMMARY.
(Erase heading not required.)

D.A.D.V.S.
61st
DIVISION

Date 15/6/18

Place	Date	Hour	Summary of Events and Information	Remarks and references to Appendices
LAMBRES.	15/6/18		Office. Visited 61st Mob Vet Sec. 61st Div Train & Dy train – 184 Bde.	JCCJ
"	16/6/18		Office. Visited 61st Mob Vet Sec. & 262 (Army) Bde R.F.A.	JCCJ
"	17/6/18		Office. Visited animals sick	JCCJ
"	18/6/18		Office. Visited 16th Div Art D.A.C. with A.D.V.S. XI Corps.	JCCJ
"	19/6/18		Office. Visited & inspected animals 183 Inf Bde. & B.A.C. g 61st D.A.C.	JCCJ
"	20/6/18		Office Visited 61st Mob Vet Sec Inspected sick animals.	JCCJ
"	21/6/18		Office Conference V.Os. of Division – Visited 61st Mob Vet Sec. Examined animals sick.	JCCJ
"	22/6/18		Office Attended Conference A.D.V.S. XI Corps. Examined animals for Evacuation	JCCJ
"	23/6/18		Office. Visited Mob Vet Sec. Examined animals & DJFR animals	JCCJ
"	24/6/18		Office India 61st Mob Vet Sec. & DJFR. animals.	JCCJ
"	25/6/18		Office. Visited & examined M.M.P. animals also 2/2 & 2/3 Field Ambulances.	JCCJ
"	26/6/18		Office Inspected DJFR. animals. Visited 61st Mob Vet Sec.	JCCJ
"	27/6/18		Office. Visited 66th D.A.C. & Dn Artillery with A.D.V.S. XI Corps. Conference of V.Os.	JCCJ
"	28/6/18		Office Visited 61st Mob Vet Sec.	JCCJ
"	29/6/18		Office & DJFR animals also animals for Evacuation at Mot Vet Sec	JCCJ
"	30/6/18		Office Examined DJFR animals.	JCCJ

J.C.C. Davis
Major A.V.C.
D.A.D.V.S. 61st Division.

Confidential.

WAR DIARY
or
INTELLIGENCE SUMMARY.
(Erase heading not required.)

Army Form C. 2118.

D.A.D.V.S. 61st DIVISION.

Date ... 1/4/18.

Instructions regarding War Diaries and Intelligence Summaries are contained in F.S. Regs., Part II. and the Staff Manual respectively. Title pages will be prepared in manuscript.

Place	Date	Hour	Summary of Events and Information	Remarks and references to Appendices
LAMBRES.	1/4/18		Office. Visited 61st D.A.C. Examined 42 Surplus Animals. Visited 61st Mob. Vet. Sec.	S.C.J.
"	2/4/18		Office. Inspected Animals 39th Batt. M. Gun. Corps. also 2/4 R. Berks. Visited 61st Mob.Vet.Sec.	S.C.J.
"	3/4/18		Office. Inspected 3rd Army Animals. Visited 61st Mob. Vet. Sec.	S.C.J.
"	4/4/18		Office. DDVS 5th Army Inspected 61st Mob.Vet.Sec.	S.C.J.
"	5/4/18		Office. Visited 476 Field Co R.E. & M.M.P. also H.Q. Company Signals.	S.C.J.
"	6/4/18		Office. Visited 61st Mob.Vet.Sec.	S.C.J.
"	7/4/18		Office. Conference with A.D.V.S. XI Corps.	S.C.J.
"	8/4/18		Office. Visited M.M.P. 61st Div. Took over duties of A.D.V.S. XI Corps while he goes on leave	S.C.J.
"	9/4/18		Office. Visited 61st Mob. Vet. Sec.	S.C.J.
"	10/4/18		Office. Visited 2/4th Division Veterinary Subsection D.A.D.V.S. also visited 61st Mob.Vet.Sec.	S.C.J.
"	11/4/18		Office. Attended Office of A.D.V.S. XI Corps.	S.C.J.
"	12/4/18		Office. Visited Office DDVS 5th Army event escort XI Corps, met him.	S.C.J.
"	13/4/18		Office. Visited 61st Mob.Vet.Sec. Attended Office A.D.V.S. XI Corps. & Vet. Evac. Station.	S.C.J.
"	14/4/18		Moved to NORRENT FONTES with Div. H.Q.	S.C.J.
NORRENT FONTES	15/4/18		Office. Inspected DTQ Animals	S.C.J.
"	16/4/18		Office. Visited Office A.D.V.S. XI Corps.	S.C.J.

Army Form C. 2118.

Confidential

WAR DIARY
or
INTELLIGENCE SUMMARY.
(Erase heading not required.)

Instructions regarding War Diaries and Intelligence Summaries are contained in F.S. Regs., Part II. and the Staff Manual respectively. Title pages will be prepared in manuscript.

A.D.V.S., 61st DIVISION. Date: 31/7/18.

Place	Date	Hour	Summary of Events and Information	Remarks and references to Appendices
NORRENT.FONTES.	17/7/18	Office.	Inspected Annuals 164 Iny Bde. — Attended Corps (XI) Conference	JRCJ
"	18/7/18	Office.		JRCJ
"	19/7/18	Office.	Conference V.O.s. of Division. Interview D.D.V.S. 5th Army re Ambulance Stripping Station	JRCJ
"	20/7/18	Office.	Visited Office A.D.V.S. XI Corps. Visited 61st Mob Vet Sec.	JRCJ
"	21/7/18	Office.	Inspected D.T.M.R. animals	JRCJ
"	22/7/18	Office.	Attended Office A.D.V.S. XI Corps, handed over on leaving Corps & Army.	JRCJ
WARDRECQUES.	23/7/18	Office.	Opened at WARDRECQUES. XV Corps. IInd Army — Visited 61 Mob Vet Sec.	JRCJ
"	24/7/18	Office.	Visited 306 Bde R.F.A. D.A.C. 61 Division. Inspected 478 & 479. Field Ors. R.S.	JFAJ
"	25/7/18	Office.	Conference V.O.s. Division. Visited 61st Mob Vet Sec.	JRCJ
"	26/7/18	Office.	Inspected C/307 & D/307 R.F.A.	JCCJ
"	27/7/18	Office.	Visited 61st Mob Vet Sec.	JRCJ
"	28/7/18	Office.	Inspect S.A.A. Sec. D.A.C. Visited Mob Vet Sec.	JRCJ
"	29/7/18	Office.	Inspected 11th Batt Supper Regt. Transport. Visited No 3 Co. 61 Dn Train	JRCJ
"	30/7/18	Office.	Inspected 164 Iny Bde H.Q. animals. Signal Sec. & M.M.P.	JRCJ
"	31/7/18	Office.	Inspected 182 Iny Bde H.Q. animals Signal Sec. also 61st Batt M.G.C. H.Q & Co.	JRCJ

J.C.C. Jones
Major AVC
D.A.D.V.T. 61 Division
B.E.F.

Confidential

WAR DIARY
or
INTELLIGENCE SUMMARY

Army Form C. 2118.

DADVS 61 Vol 28

Date 1/8/18

Place	Date	Hour	Summary of Events and Information	Remarks and references to Appendices
WARDRECQUES.	1/8/18		Office. Moved to NORRENTS FONTES. Called at Office A.D.V.S. XI Corps.	SKCJ
NORRENTS FONTES.	2/8/18		Office. Inspected M.M.P. animals.	SKCJ
"	3/8/18		Office. Inspected animals of the 1st East Lancs & 11th Suffolks	SKCJ
"	4/8/18		Office. Inspected D.T.R. animals	OKCJ
"	5/8/18		Office. Visited 6.5 Mob Vet Sec. Called at Office A.D.V.S. XI Corps.	OKCJ
"	6/8/18		Office. Visited H.Q. Quartier 5th Division - Visited 6.5 Mob Vet Sec.	OKCJ
"	7/8/18		Office - Moved with DTHQ to I.20.a.6.1. Sheet 36.A. Visited 61st Mob Vet Sec.	OKCJ
I.20.a.6.1.	8/8/18		Office. Visited Mob Vet Sec.	OKCJ
Sheet 36.A.	9/8/18		Office - Visited C.C. Machine Gun Bats.	OKCJ
"	10/8/18		Office - Visited Div Adj. Mob Vety Sec. Tho 4 Co Di Train A.S.C.	OKCJ
"	11/8/18		Office - Examined DTHQ animals	SCC
"	13/8/18		Office - Accompanied A.D.V.S. XI Corps on Inspection animals 304 Bde R.F.A.	OKCJ
"	13/8/18		Office - Accompanied A.D.V.S. XI Corps on Inspection animals 304 Bde R.F.A.	OKCJ
"	14/8/18		Office - Visited 36th Labour Group inspected animals	SKCJ
"	15/8/18		Office. DTHQ animals	OKCJ
"	16/8/18		Office. Visited DTHQ animals	OKCJ

Confidential

Army Form C. 2118.

WAR DIARY
or
INTELLIGENCE SUMMARY.
(Erase heading not required.)

D.A.D.V.S.,
61st
DIVISION.
No.
Date. 19/6/16.

Instructions regarding War Diaries and Intelligence Summaries are contained in F. S. Regs., Part II. and the Staff Manual respectively. Title pages will be prepared in manuscript.

Place	Date	Hour	Summary of Events and Information	Remarks and references to Appendices
I.20.a.6.1.	14/6/16		Office. - Scanned D.A.R. annuals	JCJ
Sheet 36 A.	16/6/16		Office. - Visited 61 Mot Vet Sec.	JCJ
"	19/6/16		Office. Inspected annuals No Q Signal Co.	JCJ
"	20/6/16		Office. Visited B/296 & C/296 Bde R.F.A. also No 1 Sec D.A.C. 39th Division	JCJ
"	21/6/16		Office	JCJ
"	22/6/16		Office. Visited 296 Bde R.F.A. with A.D.V.S. XI Corps. Inspected annuals	JCJ
"	23/6/16		Office. Visited M. Vet Sec. 61 19th annuals - Conference Veterinary Officers of Divs.	JCJ
"	24/6/16		Office. Visited Mot Vet Sec.	JCJ
"	25/6/16		Office. Inspected annuals 162 Inf Bde & No 4 Co Div Train A.S.C.	JCJ
"	26/6/16		Office. Visited H.Q. Signal Co. Scanned annuals	JCJ
"	27/6/16		Office. Visited 154 Bde H.Q. Transport. Inspected Trucks tel. Mot Vet Sec	JCJ
"	28/6/16		Office - Visited No Q Co Signals. also No 4 Co Train A.S.C. Scanned Kennels	JCJ
"	29/6/16		Office. Visited Hd Q.C. Signals. Visited 16 Labour Group & 149 Lab. Co. Scanned Horses	JCJ
"	30/6/16		Office - Conference V.Os. of Division. Scanned No Q Signal C. annuals	JCJ
"	31/6/16		Office - Visited No 2 Section of Small Arms Station 61 D.A.C.	JCJ

J.C.C. Jones.
Major A.V.C.
D.A.D.V.S. 61 Division.

Army Form C. 2118.

WAR DIARY
or
INTELLIGENCE SUMMARY.
(Erase heading not required.)

Confidential

D.A.D.V.S. 61st DIVISION.
Date 1-9-18.

Vol 29

Place	Date	Hour	Summary of Events and Information	Remarks and references to Appendices
TANNAY.	1/9/18.		Moved with Divisional Rear H.Q. from I.20.a.6.1. Sheet 36A. to TANNAY.	J.C.J.
"	2/9/18		Office. Visited D.H.Q. advanced. Gassed animals, also H.Q. Co. Signals & 61st Mot. Vet. S.	J.C.J.
"	3/9/18		Office. Visited H.Q. 1 & 2 Bns. 61 Div Train A.S.C.	J.C.J.
"	4/9/18		Office. Visited Forward Area. Gassed animals 2/3 Field Ambulance. Visited 61 Mot. Vet. Sec.	J.C.J.
"	5/9/18.		Office. Gassed animals at D.H.Q.	J.C.J.
"	6/9/18		Office. Conference V.Os. of Division. Visited Advanced H.Q. Quarrie. Gassed animals.	J.C.J.
"	7/9/18.		Office. Visited H.Q. 3 Co. Train. Inspected Remounts. Visited 2/3 Field Ambulance	J.C.J.
"	8/9/18		Office. Visited 2/3 Field Ambulance. Gassed animals.	J.C.J.
"	9/9/18		Office. Moved with D.H.Q. to CROIX. MARRAISE. Gassed D.H.Q. animals.	J.C.J.
CROIX. MARRAISE	10/9/18		Office.	J.C.J.
"	11/9/18.		Office. Visited Advanced H.Q. Gassed animals.	J.C.J.
"	12/9/18		Office. Visited Advanced H.Q. Gassed animals – Conference V.Os. of Division.	J.C.J.
"	13/9/18		Office. Visited Advanced H.Q. " " & H.Q. Co. Signals	J.C.J.
"	14/9/18		Office. Visited Advanced H.Q. " " Examined 9 D.L.L. Transport animals	J.C.J.
"	15/9/18		Office. Visited 61 Mot. Vet. Sec. & No 956. Labour Co. Inspected animals	J.C.J.
"	16/9/18			J.C.J.

Confidential

Army Form C. 2118.

Instructions regarding War Diaries and Intelligence Summaries are contained in F. S. Regs., Part II. and the Staff Manual respectively. Title pages will be prepared in manuscript.

D.A.D.V.S.,
61st DIVISION.
No. ....
Date. 1.10.18.

WAR DIARY
or
INTELLIGENCE SUMMARY.
(Erase heading not required.)

Place	Date	Hour	Summary of Events and Information	Remarks and references to Appendices
CROIX MARMAISE	15/9/18		Office. Scanned arrivals from D.T.R.	A.C.J
"	16/9/18		Office. Visited Adv M.D.Q. Scanned arrivals. 1/5 D.C.L.I. 1/4 Q.C. Signals	A.C.J
"	18/9/18		Office. Visited 61 Mob Vet Sec with A.D.V.S. II Corps. Inspected arrivals 2/2 Field	A.C.J
			Ambulance, also Horses attached Agricultural Company	J.A.C.J
	20/9/18		Office. Conference V.O.s of Division	A.C.J
	21/9/18		Office. Scanned arrivals D.T.R. Rew.	A.C.J
	22/9/18		Office. Visited Adv D.T.R. Scanned arrivals, also M.D.Q. Signal Co.	A.C.J
	23/9/18		Office. Sc D.T.R. arrivals.	A.C.J
	24/9/18		Office. Visited 2/2 Field Ambulance. Inspected arrivals N.S Company Train A.S.C.	A.C.J
	25/9/18		Office. Visited 2/1 Field Ambulance Inspected arrivals - Visited Adv M.Q. Dhalin	A.C.J
	26/9/18		Office.	A.C.J
	27/9/18		Office. Conference V.O.s of Division	A.C.J
	28/9/18		Office. Scanned M.D.Q. arrivals & M.D.Q. 61 Div Train	A.C.J
	29/9/18		Office. Visited 988 Labour Group. Advanced M.D.Q.	A.C.J
	30/9/18		Office. Inspected arrivals 306 & 307 Bdes R.F.A.	A.C.J

J.C.C. Jones
Major
D.A.D.V.S. 61 Division

Army Form C. 2118.

WAR DIARY
or
INTELLIGENCE SUMMARY.
(Erase heading not required.)

D.A.D.V.S., 61st DIVISION.
No. ....
Date 1.10.18

Nov 31

Instructions regarding War Diaries and Intelligence Summaries are contained in F. S. Regs., Part II. and the Staff Manual respectively. Title pages will be prepared in manuscript.

Place	Date	Hour	Summary of Events and Information	Remarks and references to Appendices
CROIX MARRAISE	1/10/18	Office	Assumed duties D.V. M.Q.	H.C.J
"	2/10/18	Office	Visits H.Q. 61 D.v Train	H.C.J
"	3/10/18	Office	Inspected 61 Mob Vet Sec. Compenent V.O's. Division	H.C.J
"	4/10/18	Office	Inspected animals C.R.E. H.Q	H.C.J
"	5/10/18	Office	Inspected 1st Line Transport on the march.	H.C.J
"	6/10/18		Moved with Div. H.Q. by Train to DOULLENS.	H.C.J
DOULLENS	7/10/18	Office	Opened DOULLENS. Reported to XVIII Corps. 3rd ARMY. Visited some horse lines. H.C.J	
"	8/10/18	Office	Inspected Transport on the march.	H.C.J
"	9/10/18		Moved from DOULLENS with Div. H.Q. to LAGNICOURT.	H.C.J
LAGNICOURT	10/10/18	Office	Inspected animals Div.H.Q. Visited 61 Mob Vet Sec & D.T.C Mob B.H.Q.	H.C.J
"	11/10/18	Office	Visited H.Q. & G. Signals. also Div. H.Q. Horses.	H.C.J
"	12/10/18	Office	Scanned animals at D.H.Q	H.C.J
"	13/10/18	Office	Moved with D.T.Q to NOYELLES-SUR-L'ESCAUT. Visited 61. Mob Vet Sec.	J.C.J
NOYELLES SUR L'ESCAUT	14/10/18	Office	Visited 61 Mob. Vet. Sec.	H.C.J
"	15/10/18	Office	Visited M.M.P. Inspected animals	H.C.J
"	16/10/18	Office	Inspected animals D.T.Q & some 1st Line Transport	H.C.J

WAR DIARY or **INTELLIGENCE SUMMARY**

Army Form C. 2118.

D.A.D.V.S., 61st DIVISION. No. 14-10-18.

Place	Date	Hour	Summary of Events and Information	Remarks and references to Appendices
NOYELLES-SUR-	17/10/18		Office.	JCJ
L'ESCAUT.	18/10/18		Office. Visited 3rd Q Annual Train A.S.C. Inspected 1st Line Transport animals on march	JCJ
	19/10/18		Office. Moved with Division to RIEUX.	JCJ
RIEUX.	20/10/18		Office. - Inspected 61 Mob Vet Sec.	JCJ
	21/10/18		Office. Visited 2/2 Field Ambulance Farmed animals. Visited Bde H.Q. Hosp dog Res	JCJ
	22/10/18		Office. Visited 61 Mob Vet Sec.	JCJ
	23/10/18		Office.	JCJ
	24/10/18		Moved to St AUBERT. with Div Head Quarters	JCJ
St AUBERT.	25/10/18		Office. Visited 61 Mob Vet Sec.	JCJ
	26/10/18		Moved up to VENDEGIES. Taken by Div lorry on morning of 25th inst. Visited animals in forward position. Fighting still going on, animals picketed as far as possible, but casualties likely to be large as animals are so far forward.	JCJ
VENDEGIES	"		Office. Visited 30 y Bde Wagon Lines & Company with AA & QMG animals working very hard, constantly on the road — Found Booby Trap in Office. Same Mined by Engineers — D.H.Q. Shelled during day two men wounded	JCJ
"	27/10/18		Office. Visited Several units — KHR again Shelled —	JCJ
"	28/10/18			JCJ

Army Form C. 2118.

D.A.D.V.S.,
61st
DIVISION.

No. ....
Date 29.10.18.

WAR DIARY
or
INTELLIGENCE SUMMARY.
(Erase heading not required.)

Instructions regarding War Diaries and Intelligence Summaries are contained in F. S. Regs. Part II. and the Staff Manual respectively. Title pages will be prepared in manuscript.

Place	Date	Hour	Summary of Events and Information	Remarks and references to Appendices
VENDEGIES.	29/10/18		Office. Visited by Mot. for Sec. Beaurevoir wounded twice aurivals for Evacuation. Section had	L.C.J.
"			Quiet night. VENDEGIES heavy shelling during night 28/29 estimated 1000 Gas Shells thrown	L.C.J
"			into village, many were Guard, no aurivals although in one instance shell had dropped	L.C.J
"			close to two H.Q of Bdes, no ill effects noticable —	L.C.J.
"	30/10/18		Office — Beaurevoir H.Q aurivals. Intermittent Shelling during day at times heavy	L.C.J.
"	31/10/18		Office. Visits 2/3 Field Ambulance CAMBRAI. Interviewed A.D.S. of the Division	L.C.J
"			Intermittent shelling during day. 39 aurivals Killed 745 wounded by	L.C.J
"			Shell fire during the week ending 31st inst —	L.C.J

L. C. Jones
Major
D.A.D.V.S. 61st Div.

Army Form C. 2118.

WAR DIARY
or
INTELLIGENCE SUMMARY.
(Erase heading not required.)

DADVS 61st ~~Div~~ Dw

Vol. 32

Place	Date	Hour	Summary of Events and Information	Remarks and references to Appendices
BERMERAIN	13/11		Took over duties of D.A.D.V.S.	G.H.B.
RIEUX	14/11		Attended office & duties of D.A.D.V.S., moved from BERMERAIN to RIEUX.	G.H.B.
CAMBRAI	15/11		Moved Office to CAMBRAI, attended duties of C.	G.H.B.
"	16/11		Attended duties of office	G.H.B.
"	17/11		Inspected 182 Inf Brigade & attended duties of office, visited Vivier N.b.q.r.s.	G.H.B.
"	18/11		Visited Div Signals & D.H. & Lines attended to duties of office	G.H.B.
"	19/11		Visited D.H.Q. Lines, Train H.Q. Div & attended to duties of office.	G.H.B.
"	20/11		Visited Hospitals all forces in Lines & Staffs of 306 & 307 Brigade R.F.A and attended to duties of office.	G.H.B. G.H.B.
"	21/11		Visited & inspected all forces in Lines of D.A.D.V.S. attended to duties of office	G.H.B.
"	22/11		Visited 61st D.H. & Signals, H.Q. Rgn Train & attended to duties of Office. Sent A.V.C. Clerk to D.A.D.V.S. left on 3 months leave to U.K. With 1 day late allowance for stationary, but Clerk from Base in his stead.	G.H.B.
"	23/11		Attended to duties of office & Inspected 315 Bde A.F.A.	G.H.B.
"	24/11		Office closed	G.H.B.

Army Form C. 2118.

WAR DIARY
or
INTELLIGENCE SUMMARY.
(Erase heading not required.)

Instructions regarding War Diaries and Intelligence Summaries are contained in F. S. Regs., Part II. and the Staff Manual respectively. Title pages will be prepared in manuscript.

Place	Date	Hour	Summary of Events and Information	Remarks and references to Appendices
BERNAVILLE	25/11/18		Office moved to BERNAVILLE	G.h.B.
"	26/11/18		Office closed	G.h.B.
"	27/11/18		Office reopened & attended to duties of S.A.D.V.S.	G.h.B.
"	28/11/18		Visited & inspected Lines & Horses of 306 & 307 R'de R.F.A. & 315 B'de R.F.A. attended duties of Office	G.h.B.
"	29/11/18		Visited H.Q. & Lines, also 61st Div Signal Co, & attended duties of Office 182 Inf B'de & 2/9	G.h.B.
"	30/11/18		Visited H.Q. Div Train, C.R.E., inspected horses 182 Inf B'de & 2/9 Vickers R. Transport, attended duties of Office.	G.h.B.

G.M. Bloxsome
Capt A.V.C
for S.A.D.V.S. 61st Division.

K.A.K.U.S.

61st Division No. A. 36.

War Diaries for the month of December, 1918, due in this office on 3rd instant, not yet received.

Will you please cause same to be expedited.

These have been
out dated.

[signature]
Captain,
A/D.A.A.G.
61st Division.

D. H. Q.
10-1-19.

Confidential

WAR DIARY
or
INTELLIGENCE SUMMARY.
(Erase heading not required.)

Army Form C. 2118.

D.A.D.V.S.
61st DIVISION.
No. ....
Date. 8/12/18

Instructions regarding War Diaries and Intelligence Summaries are contained in F. S. Regs., Part II. and the Staff Manual respectively. Title pages will be prepared in manuscript.

Place	Date	Hour	Summary of Events and Information	Remarks and references to Appendices
ST. RIQUIER	8/12/18		Rejoined the Division from 21 days leave to Eng. leave	O.C.J.
"	9/12/18		Office - Voted 61 Mob. Vet. Sec. Inspection Annual.	O.C.J.
"	10/12/18		Office. Inspection DHQ Animals	O.C.J.
"	11/12/18		Office. As I am without Clerk I am detained in with office work.	O.C.J.
"	12/12/18		Office. Returns	O.C.J.
"	13/12/18		Office. Weekly returns.	O.C.J.
"	14/12/18		Office	O.C.J.
"	15/12/18		Office. Visited 183 Iny Bde.	O.C.J.
"	16/12/18		Office. Inspected Hy/c. I.C. R.B. Brouwer Brook Maes.	O.C.J.
"	17/12/18		Office. Routine work.	O.C.J.
"	18/12/18		Office.	O.C.J.
"	19/12/18		Office. Conference D.D.S. of Division	O.C.J.
"	20/12/16		Office.	O.C.J.
"	21/12/18		Office.	O.C.J.
"	22/12/18		Office.	O.C.J.
"	23/12/18		Office.	O.C.J.

Confidential

Army Form C. 2118.

D.A.D.V.S.,
61st
DIVISION.
No................
Date..............

WAR DIARY
or
INTELLIGENCE SUMMARY.
(Erase heading not required.)

Instructions regarding War Diaries and Intelligence Summaries are contained in F. S. Regs. Part II. and the Staff Manual respectively. Title pages will be prepared in manuscript.

Place	Date	Hour	Summary of Events and Information	Remarks and references to Appendices
St. RICQUIER	24/12/18		Office - Saunne No Q hours of Division	A.C.J
"	25/12/18		Office Routine work.	A.C.J
"	26/12/18		Office	A.C.J
"	27/12/18		Office	A.C.J
"	28/12/18		Office	A.C.J
"	29/12/18		Office	A.C.J
"	30/12/18		Office - Examining all animals of Division for Demobilization	A.C.J
"	31/12/18		Office " "	

A.C. Jones
Major.
D.A.D.V.S. 61 Division

Confidential

WAR DIARY
or
INTELLIGENCE SUMMARY.
(Erase heading not required.)

Army Form C. 2118.

D.A.D.V.S.
61st
DIVISION.
No. ....
Date 1/1/19.

Vol 5

Place	Date	Hour	Summary of Events and Information	Remarks and references to Appendices
St RIQUIER.	1/1/19	Office.	Inspected & Classified Animals of 184 Siege Bde for Demobilization.	H.C.J
"	2/1/19	Office.	" " " " " " " " " "	H.C.J
"	3/1/19	Office.	Inspected Animals H.Q. Signals Coy for Demobilization.	H.C.J
"	4/1/19	Office.	" " 2/3 Field Ambulance — H.Q. & Divisional Train. 479 F.C. R.E.	H.C.J
"	5/1/19	Office.	" " 304 Bde R.F.A. H.Q.	H.C.J
"	6/1/19	Office.	" " 304 Bde Completed Inspection.	H.C.J
"	7/1/19	Office.	" " 306 Bde R.F.A.	H.C.J
"	8/1/19	Office.		H.C.J
"	9/1/19	Office.	Inspected Animals 61 D.A.C. for Classification.	H.C.J
"	10/1/19	Office.	Continues with inspection 61 DAC	H.C.J
"	11/1/19	Office.	Inspected Animals No. 1 Co. Train. A.S.C.	H.C.J
"	12/1/19	Office.	Inspected H.Q. Animals 61 Division.	H.C.J
"	13/1/19	Office.	Inspected Animals 315 Army Bde R.F.A.	H.C.J
"	14/1/19	Office.	Inspected C.R.O. Battery Animals 91st Bde R.F.A.	H.C.J
"	15/1/19	Office.	Inspected Animals 61 Belt Machine Gun Corps	H.C.J
"	16/1/19	Office.	Inspected Animals 446 F.C. R.E. & 2/2 F. Ambulance	H.C.J

Army Form C. 2118.

D.A.D.V.S.
61st DIVISION.
No. ......
Date. 14/2/19

WAR DIARY
or
INTELLIGENCE SUMMARY.
(Erase heading not required.)

Instructions regarding War Diaries and Intelligence Summaries are contained in F. S. Regs. Part II. and the Staff Manual respectively. Title pages will be prepared in manuscript.

Place	Date	Hour	Summary of Events and Information	Remarks and references to Appendices
S. RIQUIER	18/1/19	Office	Scanned Annuals 1st Batt. E. Lancs.	H.C.J
"	19/1/19	Office	Inspected Animals No 2 Co Train A.S.C.	H.C.J
"	19/1/19	Office		H.C.J
"	20/1/19	Office		H.C.J
"	21/1/19	Office	Commenced Inspection 162 Inf Bde Animals for Demobilisation	H.C.J
"	22/1/19	Office	Completed Inspection Animals 162 Inf Bde	H.C.J
"	23/1/19	Office		H.C.J
"	24/1/19	Office		H.C.J
"	25/1/19	Office		H.C.J
"	26/1/19	Office		H.C.J
"	27/1/19	Office		H.C.J
"	28/1/19	Office		H.C.J
"	29/1/19	Office		H.C.J
"	30/1/19	Office	Scanned Animals C.R.E. H.Q.	H.C.J
"	31/1/19	Office	Inspected Animals 61 Mot Sup Col	H.C.J

J.E.C.Jones
Major
D.A.D.V.S. 61st Division.

WAR DIARY
INTELLIGENCE SUMMARY

Army Form C. 2118.

D.A.D.V.S.
61st DIVISION
Date 1/2/19

Place	Date	Hour	Summary of Events and Information	Remarks and references to Appendices
St. RIQUIER	1/2/19	Office	Examine DTR annuals	ACJ
"	2/2/19	Office	Drawing curling work	ACJ
"	3/2/19	Office	Examined annuals DTR	ACJ
"	4/2/19	Office	"	ACJ
"	5/2/19	Office	"	ACJ
"	6/2/19	Office	Examined annuals DTR	ACJ
"	7/2/19	Office	"	ACJ
"	8/2/19	Office	Visited by Mr. Vet Laihus	ACJ
"	9/2/19	Office	Examined annuals DTR	ACJ
"	10/2/19	Office	"	ACJ
"	11/2/19	Office	Examined annuals DTR	ACJ
"	12/2/19	Office	"	ACJ
"	13/2/19	Office	"	ACJ
"	14/2/19	Office	Examined DTR annuals	ACJ
"	15/2/19	Office	"	ACJ
"	16/2/19	Office	Examined annuals DTR	ACJ

WAR DIARY
or
INTELLIGENCE SUMMARY.
(Erase heading not required.)

Army Form C. 2118.

D.A.D.V.S., 61st DIVISION.

Place	Date	Hour	Summary of Events and Information	Remarks and references to Appendices
St. RIQUIER	17/2/19	Office	Routine work.	DtCJ
"	18/2/19	Office	"	DtCJ
"	19/2/19	Office	"	DtCJ
"	20/2/19	Office	"	DtCJ
"	21/2/19	Office	"	DtCJ
"	22/2/19	Office	"	DtCJ
"	23/2/19	Office	" Visited 2 Co. 61st Div Train R.A.S.C	DtCJ
"	24/2/19	Office	"	DtCJ
"	25/2/19	Office	"	DtCJ
"	26/2/19	Office	"	DtCJ
"	27/2/19	Office	"	DtCJ
"	28/2/19	Office	" Visited 2 Co. 61st Div Train R.A.S.C	DtCJ

H. C. Jones
Major
D.A.D.V.S. 61 Division

WAR DIARY
INTELLIGENCE SUMMARY.
(Erase heading not required.)

Army Form C. 2118.

D.A.D.V.S., 61st DIVISION. Date 1/3/19

Vol. 36

Instructions regarding War Diaries and Intelligence Summaries are contained in F. S. Regs., Part II. and the Staff Manual respectively. Title pages will be prepared in manuscript.

Place	Date	Hour	Summary of Events and Information	Remarks and references to Appendices
S-RIQUIER.	1/3/19	Office	Ordinary Routine Duties.	S.C.J
"	2/3/19	Office	Examined H.Q. Animals 61 Division	S.C.J
"	3/3/19	Office	"	S.C.J
"	4/3/19	Office	"	S.C.J
"	5/3/19	Office.	Examined H.Q. Animals & Mules H.Q. Signal Co.	S.C.J
"	6/3/19	Office	Ordinary Routine Wk.	S.C.J
"	7/3/19	Office	"	S.C.J
"	8/3/19	Office	"	S.C.J
"	9/3/19	Office	"	S.C.J
"	10/3/19	Office	"	S.C.J
"	11/3/19	Office	"	S.C.J
"	12/3/19	Office	"	S.C.J
"	13/3/19	Office	"	S.C.J
"	14/3/19	Office	"	S.C.J
"	15/3/19	Office	"	S.C.J
"	16/3/19	Office	" Mule 61 Mot. M.T. Sec.	S.C.J

WAR DIARY
or
INTELLIGENCE SUMMARY

Army Form C. 2118.

Date: 14.3.19

Place	Date	Hour	Summary of Events and Information	Remarks and references to Appendices
St. RIQUIER.	17/3/19	Office	M.G.D.M.T.S.	S.C.J
"	18/3/19	Office	Cap. Blanc conu. proceeded to England for demobilization	H.C.J.
"	19/3/19	Office	Routine work.	S.C.J
"	20/3/19	Office	"	H.C.J
"	21/3/19	Office	"	H.C.J
"	22/3/19	Office	"	H.C.J
"	23/3/19	Office	"	H.C.J
"	24/3/19	Office	Moved with D.H.Q. to LE TRESPORT.	H.C.J.
LE TRESPORT.	25/3/19	Office	D.H.Q. animals marched & inspected them in the church "looking well"	H.C.J
"	26/3/19	Office	Examined D.H.Q. animals - Stables - also M.M.P. & No.2 Signal Co.	H.C.J
"	27/3/19	Office	Routine work.	H.C.J
"	28/3/19	Office	Visited N°. 4 Co. 61 Div Train R.A.S.C. Examined animals	H.C.J.
"	29/3/19	Office	Examined H.Q. & Horses 61 Div.	H.C.J
"	30/3/19	Office	Routine work. Examined N°2 & Horses	H.C.J
"	31/3/19	Office	Visited 184 Inf Bde - 1/1 & 1/2 Field Ambulances	H.C.J

L.C. Ivers
Major D.A.D.V.S. 61 Div

www.ingramcontent.com/pod-product-compliance
Lightning Source LLC
Chambersburg PA
CBHW081440160426
43193CB00013B/2335